MW00564533

'Women's Water Polo team at practice [#129]', by Sean Fornelli, (2008). [see p.211].

How To Play

WATER POLO

The Complete Guide to Mastering the Game

By
Dr Tracy Rockwell

Pegasus Publishing

Pegasus Publishing (NSW)
is a subsidiary of
Ashnong Pty Ltd

Enquiries:
P.O. Box 980, Edgecliff, NSW, Australia, 2027
www.linkageinc.co
Orders: pegasuspublishing@iinet.net.au

HOW TO PLAY WATER POLO:
The Complete Guide To Mastering The Game

ISBN: 978-0-9942014-1-6

Front Cover Image:

'DFC Sète's Dražen Kujačić prepares to throw the ball in their quarter-final against FNC Douai of the 2014 League Cup at the Georges Vallerey swimming pool in Paris', by Marie-Lan Nguyen (15 March 2014). Available at [https://commons.wikimedia.org/wiki/File:DFC_Sete_v_FNC_Douai_Coupe_de_la_Ligue_2014_t140138.jpg] under the Creative Commons Attribution 3.0 Unported license. Full terms at http://creativecommons.org/licenses/by/2.0.

Play Water Polo [eBook Version]
ISBN: 978-0-9942014-0-9
An earlier version of this book was published in eBook format, which features over
50 short video clips of featured water polo skills, and
can be downloaded from Apple iBooks at:
itunes.apple.com/us/book/play-water-polo/id992831448?mt

How To Play
WATER POLO
The Complete Guide to Mastering the Game

By
Dr Tracy Rockwell

Pegasus Publishing

CONTENTS

PREFACE

This book has been developed for an international readership as beginners across the world are still beginners, regardless of where they play. Having been involved in the game of water polo for over 50 years, it made good sense to deposit my accumulated water polo knowledge and experience in this book. After competing at both national and international level, my experience as a junior and senior representative has served me well over time to be able to maintain a presence in this great sport. But it is perhaps the experience I've accumulated as a teacher and coach that have been primarily responsible for this publication.

The stimulation for writing this guide and its predecessor 'Play Water Polo' (eBook format), was that after being hired to coach junior girls water polo at a private school in Sydney, Australia, I realised that better water polo resources were required to explain the finer points of the game to beginners. Through a futile process of searching for suitable materials, I resolved to author my own 'how to play' book for those who were interested in learning more about our great game of water polo.

In preparing this guide, many thanks are due to a number of close friends including John and Lindsay Cotterill, Will Cotterill, Johnno Cotterill, Lachlan Hollis, Paul Armstrong and members of the Sydney University 18A's Men's Water Polo Team Sydney, Australia. Thanks are also due to the various photographers attributed individually

on their respective pages and in the appendix, who were kind enough to grant copyright free licenses for their stunning water polo images.

Finally, I dedicate this book to the many passionate and committed coaches of our great game who, often without acknowledgment, toil for years on end, purely for the satisfaction of improving and guiding the development of players.

Dr Tracy Rockwell
(Dip Teach; B.Sc; M.Sc; PhD).

INTRODUCTION

This complete water polo guide was developed as a resource for both players and coaches and presents an ample variety of skills, tips and tricks to improve and master performance. 'How To Play Water Polo' builds upon the accumulated knowledge of many talented players and coaches over generations, and sequentially covers all the necessary components of the game. The book is organised progressively with water polo competence being presented by way of a structured sequence of skills ranging from easy to more difficult and challenging, with the attainment of each individual skill being built upon in the learning of the next.

Utilised as a resource, the player-centred approach provides a valuable compendium for the development of players as they are always able to improve no matter where they happen to be on the learning curve. Each skill is given a rationale as to why, how and when they should be used in play. The contents includes chapters on the history of the game; fundamentals of the game; swimming skills; ball handling skills; passing and catching skills; keeping possession; defensive skills; offensive skills; shooting skills; goalkeeping skills; and water polo tips and tricks, with each of the 11 chapters culminating in a handy checklist for monitoring and recording personal progress.

Coaches will also find the content of this book to be of exceptional benefit, especially when programming and planning training sessions, and can be confident that as a one stop practical guide the individual skills presented herein are approached in a progressive and sequential fashion.

With more than 100 skills, techniques and tips, presented by way of over 190 full color images and accompanied by easy to follow directions, 'How To Play Water Polo' presents everything you need to know about playing the great and popular game of water polo, and is a must have publication for water polo enthusiasts looking to improve and perfect their game.

Water polo was sometimes played for entertainment in kayaks on the Serpentine in London, c.1883.

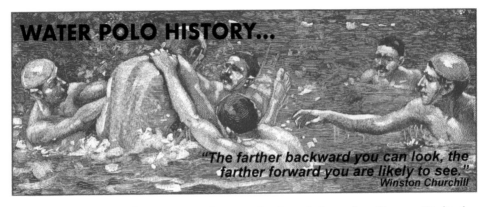

WATER POLO HISTORY...

"The farther backward you can look, the farther forward you are likely to see."
Winston Churchill

The game of water polo made its debut in Great Britain in the late 1860's, but changed frequently at the outset and over time was gradually adopted by other countries. The very early games were conducted well before any regulating or controlling body came into existence, so official documentation about the inauguration of the sport is rare. Whilst some of the facts are clear, at that very early stage in the development of aquatics, no one could foresee the popularity that swimming and water polo would create amongst people across the globe.

A Hazy Beginning

Just as competitive swimming developed slowly with occasional advances and adjustments in style and technique, so too did the sport of water polo. Of course, participation has always been limited to those who could swim, and in the early days no one documented the development of the sport. However, a number of different versions of how water polo developed have been reported and published.

One account has it that water polo was originally known as 'aquatic polo' and evolved in England in the 1860's following on from the 'Water Derbies'. In the 'Derbies' contestants were mounted on wooden barrels fitted with a rough facsimile of a horse's head and somehow participants battled over a ball in a lake or shallow water.

Another account of the origin of water polo claims that the sport began in the rivers and lakes of mid-nineteenth century England as an aquatic version of rugby football. Other theories concerning the origins of water polo are:

"In the 1860's, and possibly before that, primitive games of 'water football' were played in rivers and lakes in Great Britain. But it wasn't until 1870 that the London Swimming Association drew up official rules to govern the game. Originally it was thought that the game would provide something new for swimming gala's." (USA Water Polo Website, 2005).

"Water polo was invented in England specifically for the purpose of attracting spectators to swimming competitions. Swimming promoters conceived the idea of football in the water with the rules based on soccer, using an inflated rubber ball. In the beginning there were few rules, the main aim being to score goals by fair means or foul. Early games often deteriorated into wrestling matches; Committee members of the London Swimming Club laid down the first written rules with the aim of making the game cleaner and more free flowing. Originally, teams consisted of 3 players. Water Polo caught the attention of the media when a game was organised by the Bournemouth Premier Rowing Club, and although the ball burst during the match, the players continued to play. The field was marked by four flags tied 50 yards apart with goals being scored by placing the ball onto floating platforms." (Australian Water Polo Website, 2003).

As both of the above explanations were written relatively recently, it is interesting to compare these accounts with others penned by observers who lived a little closer in time to the beginnings of the sport.

How To Play Water Polo by 'The Captain'

"The game of "football in the water" was founded by Mr. William Wilson of London in 1844, and became known as water polo. Goal posts were not used at first and the method of scoring was to swim with the ball and place it on a floating platform at the end of the field of play. The ball was of thin rubber and was often torn to pieces, as once having gained possession of the ball,

▶Left: *An 1877 portrait of William Wilson from Scotland who drew up a set of rules for a water game, termed 'aquatic football' which took place from bank to bank at the Bon Accord Club festival. Right: This English 'Aquatic Entertainment' poster from September 14th 1877 lists an 'Aquatic Polo Match' to conclude the program at Brighton West Pier.*

the sole idea was apparently to get it to the floating platform. How the players reached their object was of minor importance and roughness was a necessary adjunct. Forty years after the formulation of the game, Mr. W. Henry, of the Royal Life Saving Society of England, standardised the game and in 1885 the English Amateur Swimming Association formulated rules and recognised the game, which immediately came under their jurisdiction. In 1888, Mr. A. Sinclair founded the London Water Polo League, with the avowed object of popularising the game. This league still occupies a leading position and has over 100 clubs and associations affiliated to it. The first international match was played at Kensington, England in 1890 between England and Scotland. Only a few countries played matches until the Olympic Federation included water polo. (The Referee, 20th October 1938, p.17).

The game had its origins in a slump in swimming and was:

"invented by a number of aquatic sportsmen, who wished to revive interest in swimming by relieving the boredom of spectators having to watch incessant swimming races." (David Barr, 1960).

Making it all the more difficult to unravel, are the mention of different names, locations and even countries. Importantly however, these and other accounts all agree that water polo was primarily developed to provide a new form of entertainment at aquatic carnivals. These almost 'prehistoric' games were

A WATER-POLO MATCH AT THE CROWN BATHS, KENNINGTON OVAL

Engraving depicting a scene of the varsity game between Oxford vs Cambridge that took place October 1891 at the Crown Baths, Kennington Oval. Due to the cold water and the lack of a covered pool in Cambridge the match had to be held in London.

▶Engraving from the Illustrated London News dated 1897 showing a Water Polo match held during a Ladies night organized at the Bath Club of London. Notice how the onlookers on the pool-deck were supplied with a canvas shiled to protect them from being splashed by the participants.

played at a time when even the great grandparents of most of today's players are now long gone. Since those early days, almost one hundred and fifty years of water polo history has left a fascinating legacy.

The Origins Of Water Polo

The actual origin of water polo appears to be that, prior to 1870, various attempts were made by individuals to arrange some kind of ball game in the water. At many aquatic exhibitions and swimming matches a game known as, 'water hand ball' was often played, with the teams usually consisting of not more than three players, but matches were also played at the time in canoes and kayaks.

In order to clarify the rules for these three sided contests, a committee was appointed by the London Swimming Association which met on 12th May, 1870, to draw up a code of rules for the management of a game they called 'football in the water.'

The frequency of matches increased after 1870, but it is difficult to obtain definite particulars as few games were reported except for a match played at a swimming fete in Victoria Park, London in 1875, and another by a rowing club at Bournemouth in England who organised a game in 1876. A newspaper of that period reported that the Bournemouth Premier Rowing Club carried out the first series of 'aquatic hand ball matches' on Thursday, 13th July 1876, off the Bournemouth Pier. Curiously enough, there were seven competitors on each side, and the goals were marked by four flags, moored at the west of the pier some fifty yards apart. The news report stated that after a "severe struggle the ball burst, but the players who were undaunted, and properly habituated, displayed their aquatic accomplishments for some time". One week later another article informed the public that...

"twelve members of the club proceeded in rowing galleys, and took up a position near their goals, which were marked out by flags describing an oblong of sixty yards by forty yards. All being ready, an India rubber ball, evidently the inside of an ordinary foot ball, was placed in the centre between the parties, and a signal given, upon which both crews sprang with commendable agility from their galleys and struck out for the ball of contention." (Unreferenced News cutting, July 1876).

The report went on to describe the subsequent match or 'battle'...

"one player got a lucky hit which sent the ball back from his goal several yards, and it seemed as if his crew were, for a time, to have their own way but a player on the other side, who instead of jumping in with his party, in the first instance, remained at his goal as backstock, now plunged in and reinforced his crew, who, after a short but obdurate tussle, turned the tide again in their favour. Again the ball burst, and, another not being forthcoming, the game was suspended."

In these pioneering games it is interesting to note the length of the field of play, the size of the goals, the thin rubber ball that could not last through the severe 'castigation' it received, and the term 'backstock' for goalkeeper, which was evidently coined from the writer's own imagination.

Initially there were no printed rules and water polo was far from the technical and sophisticated game we know

The Bournemouth Premier Rowing Club (UK) carried out one of the first series of 'aquatic hand ball matches' on Thursday, 13th July 1876, off the Bournemouth Pier, England.

today. It was instead a contest of close formations and fierce scrimmages. At first, players scored by planting the ball on the end of the pool with both hands. Early games were generally exhibitions of brute strength and aquatic wrestling. Passing and dribbling were scarcely practiced and rarely attempted. Games were fought along individual lines, that is to say, that without regard to position, each player considered it his sole duty to score goals. Games were often nothing more than gang fights in the water as players often ignored the ball, preferring instead to engage in underwater wrestling matches rather than score goals.

In many of these underwater battles, men let go of one another only when one was no longer able to endure without air and victims often floated to the surface in need of resuscitation. The goalkeeper was permitted to stand on the pool deck and protect his goal as he saw fit. If an opponent came too near the goal, he was promptly jumped on by the goalkeeper, the forwards sometimes nearly having their neck broken by the goalie jumping in on top of them.

At other times, when opponents were trying to score, the goalkeeper would lay hold of their hands and the ball, and drag them completely out of the water.

The First Water Polo Rules

The first games were played with a small 'India rubber hand ball', about four or five inches in diameter. The term polo originated from the vulcanized India rubber ball, which was used in these early games. Apart from the Hindi word 'pulu', there is no historical connection between water polo and the game of polo as played on horseback.

To begin with, the water polo goals were placed at the ends of the bath and the goalkeeper stood on the side. In 1879, the width of the goals were limited to fourteen feet and sometimes the captain ordered two goalkeepers to keep watch according to the width of the bath. At the start of play the teams stood at the ends and the ball was thrown

◄Early water polo techniques showing the back throw, the pass back, the breast-stroke pass, the overarm pass and the shoulder throw. In 'Swimming As An Art' by A. Sinclair & W. Henry, London (1893).

into the centre. In those days the water was not overly clean and a favorite trick was to place the ball inside ones bathing suit and swim under water to appear at the other end. To swim underwater during those times would have been a real achievement as the pools had no filtration systems and were dirty and cloudy most of the time.

The Pioneer Nations

The English Game (UK)

Following the well documented match off Bournemouth Pier in 1876, the English swimming clubs began to play a crude style of water polo. The Birmingham Leander Club, which was founded in 1877, and the Burton-on-Trent Amateur Swimming Club, which commenced the following year, were the first two clubs to adopt the new ball game. Teams in 1879 consisted of about nine players on each side. The Dudley Swimming Club began playing Henley in England about that year, and a season or two later the positions of the players copied the Association Football system.

In the meantime, as certain individual clubs had made up rules of their own, an attempt was made by Mr. William Henry to induce the Swimming Association of Great Britain, to recognize the game and to formulate a proper set of rules for general use amongst the clubs. Unfortunately, no initial support was accorded to the proposition at that stage.

However, the Midlanders were very keen on the sport and on 20th May 1884, a meeting of the clubs in their district was held at Burton-on-Trent and a resolution reached. It stated that a Midland Counties Swimming and Aquatic Football Association be formed, the chief object being the promotion of the game of water polo in the Midlands. This decided action induced the Swimming Association of Great Britain to reconsider their previous determination and in 1885 they passed a set of rules and recognized the game as falling under their jurisdiction.

In June 1883, a special match was arranged between the Leander and All-England clubs, the latter side winning (1~0). In the following year, All-England captained by G.R. Bettinson (Regent Club) again beat Birmingham Leander (2~0) and in 1885 defeated the Midland Counties Amateur Swimming Association by two 'touchdowns' to nothing. On these occasions the 1885 rules were observed.

A closer examination of the 1885 rules shows how primitive they were in conception and yet elegantly simple when compared with those of the present day. The ball was not allowed to be thrown, the players having to swim with it in their hands or push it in front of them. In order to obtain a goal it was necessary for the team to press down in full force with one of the players holding the ball while the rest of his team closed round him so as to prevent the ball being secured by the opposing side.

In England, it was these same rules that almost led to a fatal accident at Portsmouth. The game in which Mr. J.L. Mayger (a well known rugby player) nearly lost his life occurred in the second match between the All-England and

The very "latest thing out" in games is, we are given to understand, a pleasant pastime known as water-polo. It is easy of description. Instead of the turf at Hurlingham, Lillie Bridge, Windsor Park, or anywhere else you please, take the Thames at Maidenhead, just opposite Skindles' Lawn; instead of ponies take canoes; instead of clubs, paddles; instead of a ball, a large bung of cork or some equally buoyant substance, and then you have water-polo.

SWIMMING FÊTE IN VICTORIA PARK.

On Saturday afternoon the London Swimming Club held a fête in the bathing lake of Victoria Park, carried by Harry Parker from a boat. The fête concluded with an exciting game of water polo, in which there were eight players on each side, one side being distinguished from the other by means of a red cap. The ball, which seemed rather larger than an ordinary foot-ball, was knocked about for several minutes in the oddest manner, throwing being prohibited, and the players and the spectators seemed equally to enjoy the scramble and fun.

◄English newspapers describing very early events in the sport of water polo. Showing two versions of 'polo in the water' developed in the 1870's, the aim of both being to entice and entertain spectators at the early 'swimming carnivals'. Above: 'Canoe polo' in Western Daily Press [England], 16th June 1875, p3; Below: 'Water polo' in London Daily News, 21st June 1875, p.2.

Birmingham Leander clubs.

"A fierce struggle took place near the Leander goal, which was a heavy pontoon moored against the side of a gunboat. The tide was flowing in that direction, and Mr. Mayger, who was playing for All-Englands, was in a scrimmage pushed beneath the surface and under the pontoon. The rest of the swimmers, in their frantic efforts to gain a goal, prevented him from getting clear. It was only when nearly insensible that his rescue was effected." (Unreferenced & Undated English News cutting).

The game progressed little until the end of 1887, as the English governing body was engaged in perpetual wrangling as to the definition of 'amateur'. However, early in 1888 a committee was appointed consisting of T. Young (Richmond), H. G. Hackell and W. Henry who were charged with the responsibility of revising the laws and they compiled

LA TECHNIQUE DU WATER-POLO

Le jeu de water-polo; la position des joueurs

French publication from 1910 showing player positions on the water polo field.

a set of conditions for water polo championships. Their report was presented in April 1888 and unanimously adopted.

The new laws provided that goal-posts be eight feet wide, with a cross-bar six feet above the surface of the water and fixed at least one foot from the end of the bath. Another significant change was that the players should actually be swimming when passing or playing the ball.

Around the early to mid 1880's, as the aquatic carnivals became a popular form of entertainment, entrepreneurs quickly realised that there was money to be made from exhibitions of aquatic feats, which gradually took on more of an entertainment focus. As well as learn-to-swim programs and swim coaching, proprietors of aquatic venues understood that they could significantly increase their earnings. By featuring a water polo match, these baths proprietors generally increased their gate receipts when conducting swimming and aquatic carnivals and pageants.

By the mid 1880's the game was expanding rapidly in England and although entries for the first English Water Polo Championship in 1888 were not numerous, it was a significant development. After the preliminary rounds of the inaugural championship were completed, the Otter, Tadpole, Nautilus (all from London) and the Burton-on-Trent Amateur Club from the Midlands remained in the semi-final round. Nautilus was defeated by Burton-on-Trent (0~1) and as the Tadpoles forfeited, the famous Otter Club and the crack Burton combination were left to battle out the inaugural final. They met at the Lambeth Baths in London, with the game ending in an easy victory for the Midlanders (3~0), which resulted in the very first English water polo premiership.

◄In early matches a goal could be obtained by the ball being taken up by the hand and fairly placed on a floating stage, or boat provided for that purpose'. Drawing from 'Spalding's Athletic Library, "Water Polo" (USW Ed.) held in the E.S. Marks Collection, Mitchell Library, Sydney.

▶ *1899 Magyar Uszo Egyesulet (MUE). Amongst the first European nations to adopt water polo was Hungary, who since that time have accummulated more championships than any other country.*

The Scottish Game (UK)

It is unclear whether the events in England inspired action in Scotland, whether they occurred in isolation or whether one was stimulated by the other. However, in 1877 Mr. William Wilson, who had drawn up some rules for the Aberdeen Club of Glasgow, was asked whether the monotony of swimming racing could be varied by introducing an aquatic game to amuse spectators. The suggestion was acted upon and Mr. Wilson drew up a set of rules for a water game, termed 'aquatic football', which took place from bank to bank at the Bon Accord Club festival. Later that same year, the West of Scotland club played a game at the Victoria Baths, on the occasion of the opening of the Aberdeen Club's new natatorium. In October of the same year the rules were revised and a competition, which extended over two nights, was decided at Paisley Baths between the West of Scotland and Paisley Clubs.

The rules were again revised the next year for the Carnegie Club, after which the West of Scotland paid some attention to the game. There were no goal posts at first, the ball having to be played between two small flags placed eight or ten feet apart, and the game was merely a rough

and tumble scramble from end to end.

Keen followers of the sport soon began to recognize that this new game, if properly developed, would prove of immense service to the swimming clubs in general, and in October 1879 they consulted as to possible improvements. This led to the adoption of goal-posts similar to those used in football. Under these new conditions, the main feature of the first costumed swimming entertainment ever held in Glasgow was a polo match between the West of Scotland and Clyde clubs. The teams consisted of seven players on each side and while standing on the bottom of the bath and throwing the ball with both hands was not allowed, 'ducking' was permitted!

Meanwhile, other Scottish clubs were joining in and the game gradually improved to the point where the Associated Swimming Clubs of Glasgow was formed. A committee was established to draft a set of rules for the proper governance of the game of water polo, and a cup was presented for a new competition. The inaugural Scottish Association contest was decided upon in 1886 with the first championship winning team being the West of Scotland club.

The Irish & Welsh Game (UK)

The Irish swimming clubs developed two quite different sets of water polo rules. Those in use at Belfast were an amalgamation of the English and Scottish rules, but those adopted by the Sandycove and Blackrock clubs of Dublin were totally different. In Dublin, players were not allowed to throw the ball at goal, but had to force it with their hands against a painted mark at the end of the pool or bath.

During the mid 1880's, the game of water polo was revolutionised in Ireland by the introduction of the 'Trudgen stroke', a much faster swimming stroke that

Images of early water polo teams and matches. Opposite page: #1-1888 - Burton SC Water Polo team. #2-1889 - Edinburgh University Water Polo team. #3-The water polo team of Christchurch, NZ who were premiers from 1891 to 1893 and again in 1895. #4- The New South Wales (Australia) water polo team of 1894 that defeated New Zealand in Auckland (5~0). Above: #5-1895 - New York Athletic Club Water Polo team. #6-The team of Eastern Province, South Africa that took part in the 1900 'Currie Cup.' #7-1908 Water polo match underway in Barcelona, Spain. #8-1910 Libellule de Paris.

had been developed by John Trudgen. This new swimming technique enabled water polo to become a faster moving and more wide-open game that involved more frequent and faster swimming. Rules moved away from rugby to a soccer style of play. The goals became a cage which measured 10 x 3 feet and a goal could be scored by being thrown rather than swimming the ball into the goals. Players could only be tackled when they held the ball and the ball could no longer be taken underwater. A leather soccer ball also replaced the smaller rubber ball that had been in use up to that time.

The game also created a foothold in Wales, especially in the coal-mining centres where groups of young men used the new game to establish social clubs. Indeed, Wales competed against both Scotland and England in international competition as early as 1900.

In the latter half of the 18th century the British Empire was at its zenith and the USA as well as the new colonies in Australia, Canada, New Zealand, South Africa and elsewhere all beckoned the motherland for settlers. The new emigrants, who hoped for a better and more fulfilling life searched for opportunities in the new world, fiercely

▶First Water Polo game at the Dianabad of Wien, Austria in 1896, published within the newspaper "Illustrieerte Wiener Extrablatt" of March 14, 1896.

◄Engraving by S.T. Dodd presenting the Scotch style goalposts according to the Glasgow Organization rules of 1886 (Goal post to be 7 feet wide, 6 feet high from the surface of the water, and fixed 2 feet 6 inches from end of pond). The drawing appears in the book 'Swimming as an Art' by A. Sinclair and W. Henry, 1893).

held onto their heritage and cultural pastimes. Although the British had brutally colonised many parts of the world, they had taken with them their democratic institutions, their principles of law and religious affiliations as well as their customs, traditions and pastimes. These pastimes included many of their newly developed games and sports such as cricket, boxing, rowing, football, rugby and water polo.

The Commonwealth Nations

Water polo was quickly introduced to the British colonies and expanded by virtue of its association with the competitive swimming movement in their respective regions. To the early competitive swimmers, the game of water polo had something very distinctive about it. The game was obviously looked upon with much respect as most well organised aquatic carnivals always concluded with the 'polo match' as the grand finale. The early designation of these aquatic events as a 'carnival' is still carried on in many places and at today's swim, surf and similar aquatic competitions.

1. Australia

On the 3rd of March 1879, a small news item concerning the arrival from London of a 'Professor' Fred Cavill and his family in Melbourne was published, along with the earliest known reference to the contesting of an 'aquatic polo' match in Australia, the first to be held outside the UK.

The reference to Professor Cavill is interesting for a number of reasons. The fact that he was a very well known swimmer, swimming teacher and aquatic exponent is indisputable. Cavill became the second person to swim the English Channel on the 22nd August 1877 in one of the fastest ever recorded times, but he was picked up just 50m short of the beach and his effort was not recognised.

At that time, swimming and the new game of water polo were flourishing in London and the UK. We know that Cavill had been involved in water polo in London and that the game had not previously been reported in the

A good crowd witnessed the water polo match between Balmain Swimming Club and West Sydney Swimming Club at Balmain Baths during the 1899 season in Sydney, Australia. Source: Photo Balmain SC Archives.

Australian press before Professor Cavill's arrival. Not long after his channel swim, Cavill and his family emigrated to Australia from London aboard the "SS Somersetshire" and arrived in Melbourne on the 12th February 1879.

It wasn't long thereafter that the Bendigo Advertiser reported that the game of water polo had arrived in Australia. These facts place Australia as the first country outside the United Kingdom to adopt the sport of water polo, and Professor Fred Cavill is recognised as the father of water polo in Australia.

2. Canada

In North America, water polo made its debut in Canada before it made an appearance in the United States. The Montreal Swimming Club was one of the first in Canada to adopt water polo, which saw the sport introduced into the club in 1887.

About 500 persons, including a considerable proportion of ladies, were attracted to Hegarty's Baths, St. Kilda, this afternoon by an exhibition of swimming, in which one of the principal performers was Professor Cavill, who, amongst other aquatic feats, exhibited his side stroke as used during his recent swim in the Yarra. Master Charlie Cavill and Miss Madeline Cavill, the son and daughter of the Professor—the little girl being only six years old—also showed great skill in the water. The programme was varied by the performances of Messrs. Strickland, Stabbach, Mitchell, and Steedman, the last-named of whom gave an interesting and successful exhibition of Professor Cavill's patent swimming costumes. The entertainment concluded with the game "Aquatic Polo," which created much amusement.

"Polo in the water when played between two good teams, is exceedingly interesting to watch,, and should become very popular among so many good swimmers as there are to be found in Montreal and neighbourhood. Challenges will be accepted from any clubs." (M.A.A.A., 4th August 1887).

3. New Zealand

By 1891, and very probably well before that, water polo was certainly being regularly contested on the South Island of New Zealand, when Christchurch first won the NZ Amateur Swimming Association Water Polo Championship. Christchurch also won the trophy in 1892, 1893 and in 1895 and the game has been played all across New Zealand ever since. No other information has come to light at this stage regarding where and when water polo may have first been introduced to New Zealand.

4. South Africa & Rhodesia

The Swimming South Africa website recalls that the first National Swimming Association was established in 1899 and was called the South African Amateur Swimming Union (SAASU). At that stage the only disciplines practiced were swimming and water polo, although competition had obviously been conducted between clubs prior to the formation of the SAASU. The association was definitely present in two provinces at the time, the Eastern Province and Western Province. By then however, British soldiers would most certainly have introduced the new game to maintain morale and cool off, during the Boer War.

The United States

Water polo was reportedly first introduced into America in 1888 by Englishman John Robinson, a professional swimming instructor who had been hired by the Boston Athletic Association. But there being no suitable outdoor baths, the rules were modified and altered to suit the smaller 'tanks' of athletic clubs and other swimming associations. Probably unaware of rule changes, Robinson introduced a version of the Irish game, which used the old 'football' style rules, but these soon took on their own characteristics of American football in the water. 'American style' water polo became instantly popular with swimmers and spectators alike and by the late 1890's, water polo was being played in venues like Madison Square Garden and Boston's Mechanics Hall, which attracted over 14,000 spectators to one national championship game.

The first US rules together with a drawing of the new 'American style' water polo were published in Harper's Weekly Magazine on February 28, 1891. Interestingly, American water polo was perhaps one of the roughest games ever played. Not only was holding, sinking and pulling back a legal part of the game, but wrestling holds were permitted

◀A match between two French water polo clubs in Paris at the Paris Olympic Games, 1900.

and combative techniques to use against opponents were actually printed in instructional booklets.

While the main attraction for spectators was violence and mayhem, it was nevertheless a spectacular game that featured plays like the 'flying salmon' where the player with the ball could leap fifteen feet through the air, off the backs of his teammates to score a goal over the top of the defenders.

> "Water polo has worked itself into popularity in America, but is very rough played, and has almost reached the stage attained by football there, ambulance waggons [sic.] being invariably on hand in connection with the latter game, and the drivers never have to complain of not being able to occupy their time. On April 12th the Chicago Athletic Association met the New York Club representatives for the water polo championship of America, in New York. The match was fought out amid great excitement, players and onlookers alike being worked up to a great pitch. So evenly did the rivals contest that only one goal was secured, and that by the New Yorkers. Noses were punched and copious bleeding had the effect of lending a sanguinary appearance to what should have been a friendly game, but it apparently wasn't." (The Referee, June 5th 1895).

The European Game

Around the same time water polo was spreading throughout the British colonies and the USA, a similar

A drawing retrieved from the British illustrated newspaper "The Graphic" of 14th June 1902, shows a scene of Water Polo being played in the River Mooi of South Africa, two weeks after the Boer War ended.

▶*Clubs were permitted to compete in the 1900 Olympic Games Water Polo Championship. The champions and gold medalists were Osbourne Swimming Club, from Great Britain.*

wave of popularity began to sweep across Europe, which by and large adopted the Scottish rules. Hungary first adopted water polo in 1889, Austria and Germany in 1894, France in 1895 and Belgium in 1898. As the game expanded to various parts of the world different countries developed their own peculiar variations, but in an age of 'gentility' it was generally regarded as the 'roughest game in the world.'

The Olympics & FINA

Matches were violent yet so spectacular that by the late 1890's the new aquatic pastime was one of the most popular spectator sports. In fact, by 1896 water polo was scheduled to be contested in the inaugural modern Olympic Games in Athens, but was withdrawn at the last minute.

By 1899, the popularity of water polo had become so great that along with cricket, rugby union, polo and football, it was one of the very first team sports to be added to the 1900 Olympic Games program. After the London Olympic Games in 1908, the Federation Internationale De Natation (FINA) came into existence and has regulated water polo ever since. Hungary have been by far the most successful country in the men's program with nine Olympic

◄An early match played in Berlin, Germany about 1900.

gold medals. Women's water polo was first contested at the 27th Olympic Games in Sydney (2000) with Australia the inaugural champions, but the United States women have won medals in all Olympic contests since then.

Summary

This chapter has covered the origins of the game of water polo, how it was first established and how it was adopted by various countries around the world. The next chapter explores the game of water polo itself by examining the objectives of the game, the players and their specialist positions, the fundamentals of the sport as well as the rules and the officials that administer the game.

Chapter 2
ABOUT THE GAME

'Australia vs Kazahstan at the London Olympic Games', by Matt Brown, (31 July 2012). [see p.211].

ABOUT THE GAME...

"I always turn to the sports section first. The sports page records man's accomplishments, while the front page has nothing but man's failures"
Earl Warren

Game Objectives & Strategy

Water polo is one of the most strategic ball games with many transferable mental and physical skills between other sports. It is classified as an 'invasion game', which are team games played within a certain time period, in which the purpose is to invade an opponents territory and score goals while keeping the opposing team's goals to a minimum.

Water polo is a team sport that mixes the greatest aspects of football, basketball and hockey. Like football (soccer), goalies defend a large netted goal, but water polo players are allowed to use only one hand at a time to pass or shoot the ball. Like basketball however, there are fast breaks and a set offense that uses a center 'hole' man who can either make shots or pass off to players driving towards the goal. Working to get inside water to be closer to the goal is also reminiscent of basketball.

The 'hole' player tends to be bigger and more powerful, and they usually situate themselves in front of the goal, resisting attempts by the opposition to block or push them out. Guard-like 'drivers' tend to be quicker, good ball handlers, and effective outside shooters (like 3-point shooters in basketball). Similar to field hockey, water polo is a physical game and players can be temporarily ejected into a 'penalty box' for short periods of time if the referee

▶Water polo balls have a roughened surface to assist with grip in the water. They come in two main sizes: a size 5 (68-71 cm in circumference), intended for use by men, and a size 4 (65-67 cm in circumference), intended for women. 'Italian water polo match - C.N.Salerno vs Pro Recco', by Di Iorio Gabriele, (undated). [See p.211].

deems it necessary. If possession is indecisive the referee can occasionally order a 'neutral throw' between two players who then contest for possession of the ball to restart play.

Fundamentals of the Game

Equipment

Water polo uses very little equipment although of course all participants need to wear swim suits when participating, with swim briefs being preferable to cut down on water

Players representing their country normally line up to be introduced for National and International tournaments and matches. 'Water Polo By The Sea, Bondi, Australia, 2016'.

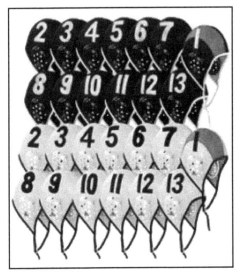

Left: Water polo teams are usually distinguished by wearing different coloured caps, usually one light and one dark set, numbered from 1 to 13. Right: Players line up ready for the swim off at the start of each 'quarter' of play.

resistance. Water polo once used old leather balls that became more waterlogged as the game went on. Today however, a rubber inflated colourful ball is commonly used, which has a slightly roughened surface for easy grip. The balls come in three separate sizes for men, women and juniors. Water polo teams are normally distinguished by the wearing of numbered and coloured caps, one set white, and the other of a different colour, while the goalkeepers must wear a red cap.

Number of Players

Although a water polo team consists of 13 people, only seven players from each team are allowed to be in the water at any one time (one goalkeeper and six in the field).

However, there has been a recent move by FINA to reduce some junior teams to 11 with only six players from each team being allowed in the water at any one time (one goalkeeper and five in the field).

Caps numbers are not generally allocated to particular players by field position except for goalkeepers who must wear the number one cap.

Positions In The Field

Water polo is a territorial game where most players are free to swim anywhere in the field of play. Some players however, are classified as holding down certain field positions by nature of the tasks they have to perform. For example, the goalkeeper is restricted to playing in their half of the field, but they are permitted to score goals. All other field players are allowed to swim anywhere in the field and score goals. Some players with certain talents, (eg. scoring goals or guarding) are often allocated to attack or defend in particular areas of the field (see Figures 2.1 & 2.2).

Apart from the goalkeeper, players are commonly assigned to play as forwards (also called drivers), halves or backs. The forwards specialise in attacking and scoring goals, with the strongest scorers placed at centre-forward (also called the 'hole'). The halves are usually proficient swimmers as their job requires them to assist or connect the goalkeeper and backs with the forwards and to help out

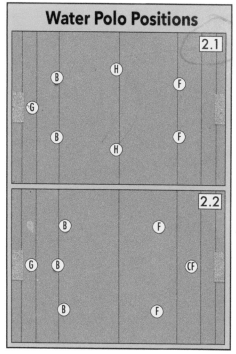

*◄Fig. 2.1 The 2-2-2 team formation suits a team of beginners, as players won't have to swim as far if they remain in their zones. The better shooters become the **F**orwards, the faster swimmers are **H**alves and the slower swimmers are **B**acks & **G**oalkeepers.*
*Fig. 2.2 The 3-3 team formation produces a stronger defensive pattern, especially with juniors, which is used to smother fast breaking swimmers, but in this scenario some of the **B**acks may also need to assist with the offense.*

▶A capable and skilled goalkeeper is a definite asset to any water polo team.

in both offensive and defensive roles. The backs specialise in slowing down and blocking any attacks on goal, with the best defender usually placed at centre-back, to mark the opposing centre-forward (hole-man). But regardless of what field position water polo players may be assigned, all team members can be required to swim anywhere at anytime.

Water polo is a body contact sport similar to basketball with a dose of wrestling thrown in. Like basketball, body contact is most intense in the centre or 'hole' where strong leaning, pushing and holding must be used to stay in position. Only one person at a time is usually in the centre position so it's easy for beginners to avoid heavy contact if they don't like it. Most shots are scored from outside the centre where body contact drops off dramatically.

Length of the Game

A game can last from around 45 to 60 minutes, but is divided into four equal quarters, which varies according to age and ability. Teams are discouraged from dominating the ball as a 30 second possession or shot timing clock is used, which gives both teams an opportunity to handle and score. Two minute intervals separate each quarter, and teams are usually allowed to take two time-outs per game. Important matches have one or two officials solely designated to control the timing aspects of each match.

Method Of Scoring

Goals are scored when the whole ball crosses the goal line. Scores are typically in the range of 6 to 14 goals per game. A good goalkeeper is an essential member of the team and is the only player allowed to touch the ball with

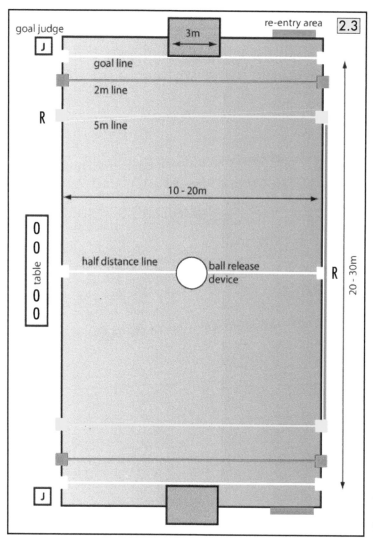

◀Fig. 2.3 The water polo field consists of a minimum width (20m) and length (25-30m) and has a number of imaginary lines that traverse the pool, which are indicated by coloured markers or lane ropes at the sides of the pool. The **R**eferees, **O**fficials and goal **J**udges are shown in this image, along with the re-entry box, where ejected players may re-enter the game.

both hands simultaneously. Although all players can score (including the goalkeeper) field players can only use one hand to touch the ball at any one time, and a goal may be scored with any part of the body, with the exception of a clenched fist!

Field Of Play

A water polo field can be any reasonable size with many games being roped off and played in rivers, lakes, harbours and the sea, but officially a water polo field should be all deep water and measure 20m wide by 30m long (FINA mens rules) or 25m long (FINA women & juniors). The size of the goal should measure 3m wide, with exactly 0.9m from the water surface to the underside of the crossbar.

Physicality

All games are refereed and excessive grabbing, pushing, or hitting of any kind is considered a foul. Like basketball

▶*A water polo referee is in full control of the game and signals the start and stop of play, all major and minor fouls, ejections and goals.*

A ball must completely cross the goal line for a goal to be scored. Left: the ball has not crossed the 'plane' of the goal frame- NO GOAL. Right: The ball has fully crossed the frame of th goal - GOAL.

or football, accidental hand or elbow contact does occur, but thankfully the water is a much more forgiving medium than a hardwood floor or a dirt field and the potential for injury in water polo is low. Beginners should be more comfortable playing water polo than if they played football or basketball.

Summary Of The Rules

A thorough examination of the rules of water polo in this book would not only be lengthy, but also difficult for most beginners to comprehend, therefore the following summarised rules of water polo are presented in a brief format.

The two referees are in complete control of all aspects of the game including scoring, timekeeping, fouling, behaviour etc. Water polo fouls are far more common than in any other sport and are part of the fabric of the game. There are two main types of infringements classified as either 'ordinary' or 'major' fouls.

Summary of Water Polo Rules

ORDINARY FOULS

There is no limit to the number of ordinary fouls a player may commit. A short summary of ordinary fouls includes:

- Grabbing, sinking or reaching over the shoulder or upper body of a player not holding the ball (If a player lifts the ball or has a hand on top of the ball, then reaching over and sinking are not fouls).
- Kicking, splashing water in the face, pushing off from a player using either hands or feet.
- Touching the ball with two hands (except the goalkeeper).
- Pushing off from the bottom, ends or sides of the pool, or off the goals.
- Attacking inside the 2m area when the ball is outside the 2m area.
- Pushing the ball underwater when being challenged.
- Wasting time when in possession of the ball.

MAJOR FOULS

Committing three major fouls in a game excludes a player from any further participation in that match.

- Reaching aggressively over the head (especially when defending the hole).
- Any ordinary foul committed by a defender when the opposing player is in a scoring position inside 5m (like fouling a 'driver' or the hole man if they have inside water).
- Blatant, aggressive fouls committed away from the action (for example, grabbing an ankle when someone is trying to swim away).
- Interfering with or blocking a free throw (the defender must allow at least 1m of space).
- A defender blocking a shot with two hands (ejection if outside 5m, penalty if inside 5m).
- A player not fully exiting the field of play before a new player can substitute is termed an illegal substitution.
- Disrespect to the referee including foul language, contesting a call, or even scowling (this is at the referee's discretion and most are extremely strict!).
- Any act of brutality such as punching or fighting (offenders can be ejected for the match, without substitute).

Ordinary Fouls

Ordinary fouls are frequently committed, which are indicated by the referee blowing their whistle and awards ing the ball to the opposing team by pointing in their attacking direction. After a foul is whistled, the team in possession of the ball is allowed a 'free throw'. Any offensive player can take the free throw, but they have roughly only three seconds to put the ball into play without interference from the defender. After a foul, the ball normally can't be shot at the goal until it has been passed to another player. An exception to this rule is when an ordinary foul is committed outside the 5m line (yellow zone), in which case a quick shot by the fouled player is permitted.

Good referees call fouls immediately whenever there is unreasonable contact, and are usually so eager to keep the game 'clean' that a whistle is blown almost every 15 seconds. But referees should do their best to keep games flowing, allow the advantage and try to ignore fouls committed away from the action so as not to interfere with possible scoring opportunities.

The Two Metre Rule

The 2 metre rule often causes confusion, but it is important to understand that this rule only applies to the attacking team. It is not an offence if a player takes the ball into the 2m area and passes it to another player who is also inside the 2m area. But any attackers inside the 2m area must retreat out of the 2m area once the ball has been passed out.

Major Fouls

Major fouls (or 'Personal Faults') usually result in an offender being given a temporary 20 second ejection foul (also called a 'kick out') in the penalty box. However if the foul occurs in the attacking zone a 5m penalty foul is awarded. If a player receives three major fouls of any kind, they are immediately ejected for the remainder of the game, but may be substituted.

Penalty Shots

A penalty shot is a contest between a designated shooter and the goalkeeper. Penalty shots are taken from the 5m line

The referees may award the taking of a penalty throw to an attacking team for a major infringement of the rules, which is taken on the 5m line by a designated player. (Use of this image is licensed under Creative Commons).

The Two Metre Rule

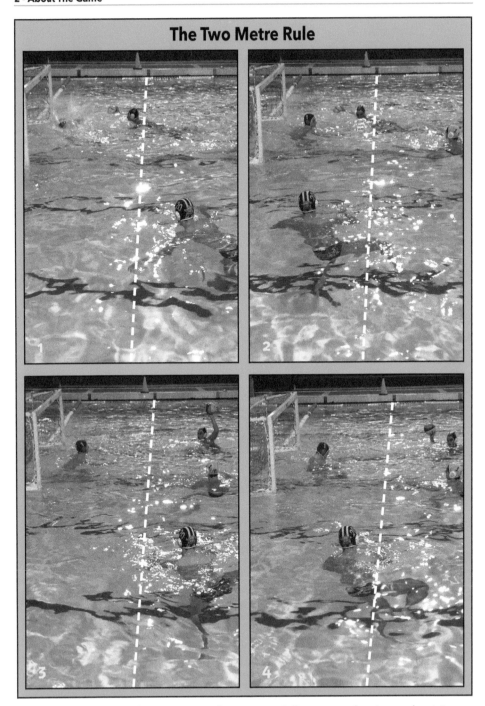

The 2 metre rule often causes confusion especially amongst beginners, but it is important to note that it only applies to the attacking team. FINA rules state that 'it is a foul to be within two metres of the opponents' goal line except when behind the line of the ball'. Therefore, it is not an offence if a player takes the ball into the 2m area to score, or to pass to another player who is also inside the 2m area and behind the line of the ball. Images 1 to 3 above are legal, while only 4 is a 2m infringement.

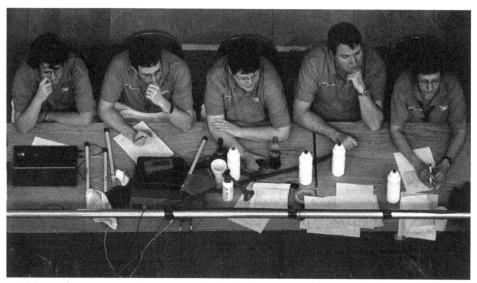

Water polo games require secretaries & timekeepers to keep track of various aspects of the game including the score, personal fouls, time-keeping, the possession clock, ejections, time-outs, substitutions etc. (Use of this image is licensed under Creative Commons).

directly in front of the goal. The referee will award a penalty if a major foul is committed when someone is in a strong, imminent scoring position in the attacking area in front of goal. For example: if the hole man or a driver has the ball and also controls 'inside water' within 5 meters of the goal, and the defender impedes by coming over their back.

Also, if a goalkeeper pushes or takes the ball underwater while being pressured, or a defender blocks the ball with two hands, then a penalty shot will be awarded to the attacking team.

Summary

This chapter has explored the different facets and rules of the game of water polo by examining the objectives of the game, the players and their specialist positions, the equipment as well as the rules and duties of the referees and officials that administer the game. The next chapter presents the necessary information and images required for learning the various swimming skills that are indispensable for learning to play the game of water polo.

◀Referee watching the clash of swimmers during a swim up at the start of play. Water polo is a competitive team sport consisting of four quarters, usually of eight minutes, in which the two teams attempt to score goals by throwing the ball into their opponent's goal. The team with the most goals at the end of the game wins the match. Each team is made up of six field players and one goalkeeper. Except for the goalkeeper, players participate in both offensive and defensive roles. The goal keeper is allowed to use two hands at all times. Water polo is typically played in an all-deep pool of at least 1.8m (6'). (Use of this image is licensed under Creative Commons).

Checklist of Water Polo Fundamentals

Skill #	Skill Name	✔	Date Mastered
1	Objectives & Strategy		
2	Fundamentals of the Game		
3	Summary of Water Polo Rules		
a	*Ordinary Fouls*		
b	*2m Foul*		
c	*Major Fouls*		
d	*Penalty Shots*		

Chapter 3
SWIMMING SKILLS

'George French (CLU) swimming in a UC Irvine vs Cal Lutheran match, score 11-5',
by Chris Hunkeler, (undated). [See p. 211].

SWIMMING SKILLS...

*"The more you sweat in practice,
the less you bleed in battle."*
Gen. George S. Patton

The Importance of Swimming Skills

Water polo is a fantastic team sport for people of all ages. It builds an appreciation of what a group can achieve when they work together as a team, and is one of the most physically demanding games ever developed. Naturally, as water polo is played entirely in deep water, some swimming ability is required. Even our great-grandfathers could see that water polo was a great way to develop swimming skills:

> *"Water Polo is essentially a game for swimmers and one that affords ample opportunity for the exhibition of skill and the development of staying power. It's practice tends to improve the speed of all those who participate in the game, as well as to develop in the minds of its followers good ideas as to the best methods of obtaining command over themselves in the water. In water polo the rapid changes of position which are necessary, compel players to constantly alter their style. This is in itself a beneficial phase of the game and one which teaches a swimmer how complete their power in the water can become." (New Zealand ASA, 1894/95 Annual, p.76).*

Water polo requires a number of different swimming strokes and styles, and contrary to popular belief, the game does develop explosive swimming speed. In fact many Olympic swimming champions having also played the game.

There are however, some very important differences between the streamlined stroke style of a competitive swimmer and the explosive skill required of a water polo player. To facilitate personal development in this sport, swimming practice for water polo players should always model the fast-paced, stop-start, back-and-forth action of a water polo game, which no amount of lap swimming can simulate.

Although butterfly can be used as an effective stroke to gain fitness, water polo players primarily use variations of freestyle, backstroke and breaststroke. The main difference being that in order to effectively play the game, a participant should be able to see the ball at all times.

They should be able to watch their teammates, keep an eye on the opposition players, the location of the goals, gauge their position in the field and watch any decisions indicated by the referees. Therefore, most of the swimming in water polo is performed by carrying the head out of the water. This chapter details the swimming skills required

To effectively play the game of water polo, a participant should be able to see the ball at all times, and especially while swimming.

for various techniques and strokes used both in training to develop fitness and in playing water polo games.

4. Sculling

As basic as it sounds, the ability to 'scull' is a critical skill for water polo players and particularly for beginners. Those who know little about the game make the common mistake of not using their hands to balance. Sculling is an essential component for being able to move, balance and create force in the water.

This skill is normally performed when treading water, but the body position varies for water polo players. As they transfer their weight further forward and elevate their hips, they need to use a more vigorous sculling action to support the upper body and head.

Begin with both hands out in front, sculling from side to side. Then lean to the left, which requires vigorous sculling with the left hand. Once mastered, try lifting the right arm out of the water. Repeat this on the right side and lift the left arm out of the water. Then repeat these two skills, but use an egg-beater kick instead of breaststroke kick or treading water.

Next, try balancing in the water in a variety of different positions both stationary and while swimming (ie. on the

Sculling

Practice:
1. Place hands out in front with palms facing down;
2. Lean forward & fan from side to side with both hands;
3. Tread water vigorously and press down on the water;
4. Alternate with left hand only, then right hand only.

Head Up Freestyle

Skill Sequence:
1. Use a short, choppy & quick stroke rate;very
2. Shorter pull through, high elbow recovery;
3. Keep the head out of the water with back arched;
4. Looking forward and use a vigorous kick action.

(Use of this image is licensed under Creative Commons).

front, side, back etc.). In all cases it helps a great deal if the hips are as high up on the surface as possible when sculling vigorously.

The real benefit of being able to scull correctly becomes evident when a player is able to support themselves with just one hand, while leaning forward in the water. With the throwing arm out of the water, sculling with the non-throwing arm creates balance while moving forward and stops the upper body and face from falling into the water.

Once this skill has been mastered, switch the hands over and repeat the same action as you move across the pool and back. After becoming more familiar with keeping yourself afloat and using sculling techniques for balance, you can introduce ball handling skills.

5. Head Up Freestyle

The most common swimming stroke used in the game of water polo is freestyle, but it is performed by carrying the head clear of the water and is known as 'head-up' freestyle. Head up freestyle is an easy adaptation of normal freestyle, which requires just a few modifications to maximise speed. However, swimming with the head out of the water takes

ANALYSIS OF HEAD UP FREESTYLE

Back & Feet:
The back must be arched and the player should employ a much more vigorous kicking action.

Arm Stroke:
The pull through the water is shorter, quicker and much more powerful with the elbows lifted higher as they recover. The stroke rate is virtually doubled.

Water Resistance:
Swimming with the head raised takes the body out of alignment, increasing water resistance.

Head Position:
The head is carried clear of the water with the eyes looking straight ahead.

Head Up Backstroke

6

Skill Sequence:
1. Head out, looking back at the feet;
2. Back rounded, use short, choppy strokes;
3. High stroke rate with a shorter pull through;
4. Vigorous kicking action.

the body out of alignment, increasing water resistance, so some adaptations need to be made to perform this stroke efficiently.

The pull through the water should be shorter, quicker and much more powerful with the elbows lifted higher as they recover. Compared to normal freestyle, the stroke rate is virtually doubled. To compensate for the added weight of lifting the head out of the water, the back should be significantly arched and the player should employ a much more vigorous kicking action. The head is carried clear of the water, but for the most part, the eyes should be looking straight ahead. Looking ahead allows performers to see what is happening ahead of them and to quickly gauge their responses to the flowing dynamics of a game.

6. Head Up Backstroke

Backstroke is another essential swimming stroke used in water polo. This stroke is used to best effect when players are attacking down field and the ball is behind them. In this instance players can roll onto their back and perform head up backstroke without losing too much speed, while maintaining eye contact with the ball.

The main modification to conventional backstroke is

that the head is lifted out of the water so that the player has a clear view of their feet and down the pool. The arm-stroke and kick are similar to backstroke, but the upper back is more rounded and the stroke rate is quickened. Once the ball catches up to or moves ahead of a player, they should roll over and continue swimming head up freestyle. A useful variation of this skill involves the use of breaststroke kick with backstroke arms, which assists with making a quick start when on the back, or when lunging to catch a high pass.

7. Stops & Starts

The ability to stop quickly and then rapidly gain sprinting speed again is a much valued skill in water polo as this change of pace constantly occurs throughout all matches, and is one of the exciting features of the game.

When performing head up freestyle a stop is best achieved by increasing resistance against the water. This can be easily effected by spreading the thighs from a streamlined to a 90^0 position, which presents an increased surface area and immediately slows down the swimmer. At the same time, the hands should extend out in front with palms pushing against the water to add to the resistance.

Stops & Starts

**Skill Sequence:**
1. Perform head up freestyle, then stop;
2. Keep the hips on the surface, and stop with palms of the hands;
3. Big breaststroke kick & short strokes to re-start;
4. Employ rapid arm-stroke to quickly speed up.

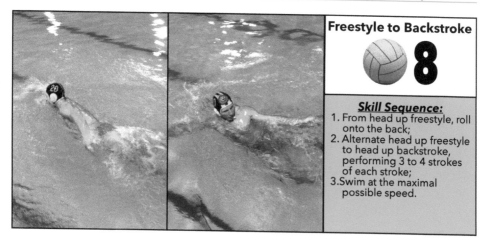

Freestyle to Backstroke

8

**Skill Sequence:**
1. From head up freestyle, roll onto the back;
2. Alternate head up freestyle to head up backstroke, performing 3 to 4 strokes of each stroke;
3. Swim at the maximal possible speed.

Then from a 'standing start' use a powerful breaststroke kick to make a surging movement before employing rapid arm strokes to get yourself up to speed again.

8. Freestyle to Backstroke

Another often used swimming technique in the game of water polo is the ability to quickly change from head up freestyle to head up backstroke and vice-versa. This adaptation is used to best effect when a player is swimming down field and the ball is behind them. By performing 'freestyle/backstroke' the player is much more able to see the ball and process the ever changing developments of the match.

To effectively perform this skill players need to be swimming down field at full speed, but should also keep their eye on the ball. Players roll onto their back and perform head up backstroke for a few short strokes without losing too much speed, before rolling back over onto their front using head up freestyle to continue the attack without losing any forward momentum.

9. Change of Direction 90⁰

The ability to rapidly change direction is another essential swimming skill for water polo. As possession changes frequently from one team to another, so too must

Changing Direction

9 & 10

Skill Sequence:
1. From Head Up Freestyle, reach back;
2. For 90° & 180° turns - dig in deep behind the hip & stop;
3. Draw the knees up to the chest, big breaststroke kick and head off in the new direction;
4. Turn the head either 90° or 180° & restart.

players be ready and able to transition from offense to defense. Swimming head up freestyle at full speed may in an instant need to change to swimming at right angles or even be reversed.

To perform a 90° change of direction (to the left), a player stops their left arm taking a forceful and deep backward stroke to prevent forward momentum. Then twist the hips and the lower body around to be in alignment with the new direction and simultaneously draw the legs up under the body. At this stage you should be facing at a 90° angle to your original direction. Then use a powerful breaststroke kick to get going from the 'standing start', and at the same time employ rapid arm strokes to get yourself back up to speed again.

10. Change of Direction 180°

To perform a 180° change of direction, a player should keep their hips closer up to the surface. Then by placing one arm behind, take a forceful and deep backward stroke to stop any forward momentum. Twist the upper body as if you were touching the wall to make a turn at the end of the pool and simultaneously draw the legs up into the body. At this stage you should be facing in exactly the opposite direction. Use rapid arm strokes to get yourself back up to speed again and a powerful breaststroke kick to get going from the 'standing start'.

A variation of this skill is to go from swimming head up freestyle to swimming head up backstroke while still facing in the same direction, or from swimming head up backstroke to swimming head up freestyle while still facing the same direction.

11. Trudgen Stroke & Breaststroke

This swimming style was named after the English swimmer John Trudgen (1852–1902) and evolved out of sidestroke. Essentially the stroke uses a head up freestyle arm action with a sidestroke scissor kick action for the legs. The kick is usually performed on every second arm stroke. In water polo this stroke is useful to maintain eye contact with the ball and with other developments occurring in a game, while still propelling yourself forward.

An effective variation of the Trudgen stroke is to perform a head up freestyle arm action combined with a breaststroke or even egg-beater kick leg action, which allows a player to make a quick and effective lunging start when necessary.

Breaststroke is a useful and popular water polo stroke as it is performed in the front position and is performed with

Trudgen Stroke

11

Skill Sequence:
1. Use Head Up Freestyle with arm stroke at a good rate;
2. Keep the back arched and use a scissor kick;
3. Look forward & kick to the dominant side;
4. Interchange with breaststroke kick to increase power.

ANALYSIS OF EGG BEATER KICK

Active Joints:
All the joints of the lower limb are active during the egg-beater kick, with the fastest movements occurring in the feet.

Alternate Legs:
Alternate circular movements of the legs to produce a strong downward force, which propels the player in an upward, forward or backward direction. When one leg is in the recovery phase, the other leg is in the power phase.

Height:
Height out of the water when using egg-beater kick is strongly related to foot speed or how quick and forceful the circling leg movements are being performed.

Circular Leg Action:
The legs move in a circular pattern and alternate during the kick with the right leg moving anti-clockwise and the left leg moving clockwise.

(Use of this image is licensed under Creative Commons).

Egg Beater Kick

12

Skill Sequence:
1. Lean forward in a sitting position;
2. Knees at 90°, with thighs parallel to the surface;
3. Legs rotate alternately inwards from the knees;
4. Increase foot speed (with toes pointed up) for lift.

the head out of the water. It is also an effective stroke for making quick starts from a 'dead' position in the water, and is easy to interchange with head up freestyle.

Due to its explosive force, breaststroke kick is particularly useful whenever a player needs to jump or lunge for the ball or to mark an opponent. Breaststroke also affords a player a good view of the water polo field and the ball. But because breaststroke is not a fast stroke it should only be used for brief resting periods, definitely not for attacking or sprinting!

12. Egg Beater Kick

Being able to master egg-beater kick is an essential skill for all water polo players. Egg-beater kick allows players to constantly keep their heads above water without expending too much energy, and provides enough stability in the water to catch, pass, shoot and defend. Egg-beater kick is a foundation skill in water polo and should be mastered before progressing to ball-handling, shooting, general offensive/defensive skills and it is absolutely essential for goalkeeping.

Egg-beater kick consists of alternating circular movements of the legs that produce a strong downward force, which propels the player in an upward, forward or backward direction. The legs move in a circular pattern and alternate during the kick with the right leg moving anti-clockwise and the left leg moving clockwise. When one leg is in the recovery phase, the other leg should be in the power phase.

All the joints of the lower limb are active during the egg-beater kick, with the fastest movements occurring in the feet. The height maintained in the egg-beater kick is strongly related to foot speed or how quick and forceful the circling leg movements are being performed.

13. Jumping

Being able to jump up and out of the water from a deep pool is another essential water polo skill. Jumping is necessary for getting yourself high out of the water to shoot, or when attempting to block a pass or a shot, and is the major skill required for making interceptions. It is also an excellent practice technique for building dynamic leg power and strength.

A jump is achieved by winding up your egg-beater kick and moving the hips close to the surface. Then attain maximal foot speed while sculling vigorously with the

Jumping

13

Skill Sequence:
1. With hips close to the surface, use a vigorous egg-beater kick;
2. Vigorous sculling with hands close to the surface & maximal foot speed;
3. With hands pushing down on the water, perform one explosive breaststroke kick;
4. Raise the left, right or both arms as needed.

'Jumping out with great egg-beater kick is Sofia Konuch of Russia', by Quelle: Eigenes Werk; ShaMan186, (4 Aug 2017). [See p. 211].

The swimming for the ball contest at the start of a match is always a highlight of this game. Learning and obtaining sound swimming skills are essential part of playing the game of water polo.

hands. A final explosive breaststroke kick and pushing down with the hands forces the body out of the water, where you are then free to raise your arms for a block or interception with either hand if necessary.

Summary

There are many other variations and adaptations of swimming skills that can be programmed and performed for water polo, but the techniques outlined in this chapter are by far the most commonly used swimming skills that have been adopted over time by water polo players. After these skills have been introduced, practiced and mastered, they form the basis of physical conditioning for all water polo athletes. In the next chapter, new recruits to water polo will learn how to combine these unique swimming skills with ball handling techniques.

Checklist of Swimming Skills

Skill #	Skill Name	✔	Date Mastered
4	Sculling		
5	Head Up Freestyle		
6	Head Up Backstroke		
7	Stops & Starts		
8	Freestyle to Backstroke		
9	Change of Direction - 90^0		
10	Change of Direction - 180^0		
11	Trudgen Stroke		
12	Egg Beater Kick		
13	Jumping		

Chapter 4
BALL HANDLING SKILLS

(Use of this image is licensed under Creative Commons).

BALL HANDLING SKILLS...

"Courage doesn't always roar, sometimes it is the little voice at the end of the day that says... 'I'll try again tomorrow'."
Mary Ann Radmacher

Why Ball Handling Skills Are Important

Being a ball sport, water polo is a game that requires excellent hand-eye co-ordination and fingertip control. Before you can master the lob shot, the backhand or a trick pass, a player should become proficient in basic ball handling skills. To accomplish this players need to practice ball handling skills over and over until they become an automatic part of their game. Practicing the skills outlined in this chapter will improve hand-eye co-ordination, reaction time, strengthen

◀Before mastering the basic catch and pass, the lob shot, the backhand or even a trick pass, a player must become proficient in basic ball handling skills.

Swimming with Ball

14

Practice:
1. Move the ball from one hand to the other, side to side;
2. Push & hold the ball under, & release;
3. Lift the ball into the air & drop on the water;
4. Swim with the ball in hand, both left & right hands, with B/K, B/R, B/F.

wrists and fingertips, develop the arms and legs and will also improve your general water polo skill level.

Ball handling skills can be as varied as your imagination allows and should be conducted both in and out of the water. The main objective is to develop a 'feel for the ball' through touching and feeling the ball. Like a skilled basketball player, being able to touch and know how the ball feels without actually looking at it allows the eyes and brain to attend to and process other stimuli. With our sense of sight unburdened by simple ball handling tasks, players free up their attention to survey the game and concentrate more on tactical and strategic decisions.

14. Swimming With The Ball

Swimming with the ball in hand (not dribbling) is a great skill to increase ball handling skills and should therefore be performed whenever practical. Understanding the 'feel' of the ball by moving it from side to side, pushing it under and releasing it to gauge its buoyancy or just making fingertip contact is essential for improving eye-hand and general ball handling skills.

Performing any stroke with the ball will increase swimming fitness and improve ball handling skill at the same time. For example, although butterfly is not used

Balancing with the Ball

15

Practice:
1. Tread water with ball, then remove one arm;
2. Body position should be leaning slightly forward;
3. Balance by sculling with the non-throwing hand;
4. Hold the ball in the other hand, move it around, spin it, pop it up etc.

in water polo, performing butterfly in training with a ball in front forces concentration to maintain control; so does swimming backstroke and dribbling the ball behind the head; or performing breaststroke with the ball in front to increase awareness and ball control.

15. Balance & The Ball

Learning to maintain balance with the ball is a much overlooked skill for beginners, as most coaches just assume that their players will 'get it' at some stage. But even before a ball is introduced, poor water balance will affect a players ability to perform skills and therefore impact upon how quickly they develop. A good starting point for developing balance with the ball is to be able to 'tread water', which involves the use of both arms and legs and then just remove one arm from the action.

When holding a ball out of the water the main balancing mechanism is to lean forward and scull with the non-throwing hand. The key difficulty in achieving this balance when holding a ball is co-ordination, but once egg-beater kick and sculling have been simultaneously mastered, greater co-ordination, balance and ball control will result.

16. Ball Control

There are many varied skills and drills that promote ball control, but virtually any skills where the hands and fingers are in close contact with the ball are beneficial.

Out of the water ball handling skills include throwing and catching with a teammate, throwing and catching off a wall, throwing the ball up in the air and catching with the dominant or non-dominant hand etc. Repeat these exercises in the water, and add alternate tapping of the ball into the air one hand after the other, keeping the ball on the fingertips (similar to a volley). Passing from the left hand to the right hand, back and forth, and alternately squeezing the ball with the left then right hands, so that it is propelled upwards are all good ball control exercises.

Other fun skills include: making the ball do circles around the head; lifting the body out of the water and making circles around the chest (with the ball going under the arms); popping the ball underwater and watching how it reacts after being released; making 'water wheels'; balancing the ball on the forehead; keeping the ball in the air by doing headers; spinning the ball on a finger; flipping it up with the

Ball Control

 16

Practice:
1. Fingertip tapping above head;
2. Left hand to right hand passing;
3. Squeezing the ball, left, right & both;
4. Perform the water wheel, with both hands;
5. Circles around the head, both hands;
6. Push the ball under and let it pop up;
7. Balance the ball on your forehead;
8. Move the ball around with your feet.

THE 'READY' POSITION

Hand out for Balance
Non-throwing shoulder and arm reaching forward and sculling to balance the body out of the water.

Co-ordination:
The main difficulty in achieving balance in the water is co-ordination, but once egg-beater kick and sculling have been simultaneously mastered, greater balance and control will result.

Elbow Clear
Throwing elbow should be well clear of the water and ready to pass or shoot.

Picking up the Ball

17

Skill Sequence:
1. Establish a balanced position, with arms apart;
2. Spread the fingers and place the hand under the ball;
3. Lift the ball out to the 'ready' to pass position.

back of your hand and then catching; and playing the ball with your feet are all fun and very challenging ball control activities. Remember that developing good ball control comes from exposure to a variety of skills with the only rule being to perform these skills and drills as frequently as possible. Play a game of water polo with feet only!

17. Picking Up The Ball

Picking the ball up off the water effectively and without fumbling can be achieved using a number of different methods. These methods vary in complexity and some are strictly for experienced players. For beginners the most reliable technique is to simply place the hand under the ball and pick it up from underneath.

a. Basic: Under-ball Pick Up

The player should first place their non-throwing hand ahead or to the side of the ball to create balance by sculling. Then whilst performing egg-beater kick place the palm of the throwing hand under the ball, spread the fingers wide, cup it (without grabbing or squeezing) and gently lift the ball out of the water. As the ball is being

◄Picking the ball up off the water without fumbling can be achieved using a number of different methods. 'Women's Water Polo team at practice [#062]', by Sean Fornelli, (31 July 2008). [See p. 211].

raised the arm rotates around 90⁰ from in front to the side of the shoulder. The ball should now be in what is known as the 'ready position', which means it is ready to be passed or thrown at the goal.

b. Easy: Roll Over & Pick Up

Place the hand on top of the ball, then roll the hand round the outside until the palm is underneath the ball so that it can be lifted into the ready position. Then use the same 'Under-ball Pick Up' as mentioned above.

c. Challenging: Push Under & Pick Up

This method of picking up the ball makes use of the buoyancy of the ball. Push the ball slightly into the water and then quickly release it, taking advantage of its buoyancy, and then again roll the hand round the outside until the palm is underneath. This action needs to be performed rapidly or as soon as the ball pops back out of the water. Once in this position simply lift the ball into the ready position as mentioned above.

d. Difficult: Assisted Pick Up

While performing head up freestyle, guide the ball from underneath with the non-throwing hand and flick it backwards onto the throwing hand. This skill also allows a player to take their eyes off the ball, pick up the ball while they are swimming, and attend to other more strategic game tasks while still maintaining ball control.

18. Transferring The Ball

Transferring the ball from the left to the right hand or vice-versa, is a necessary ball handling skill for all players as it promotes ball handling with both arms.

Keeping shoulders clear of the water, players start with the ball in front and on the water. Build to a solid egg-beater kick then place one hand under the ball. Increase foot speed in the egg-beater kick and bring the ball up to the ready position, before returning the ball back to the starting position on the water. Once this skill has been mastered just swap the hands over and repeat the skill with the non-dominant hand.

Extend this skill by flicking the ball from one hand to the other as opposition players may lunge at the ball carrier from any direction.

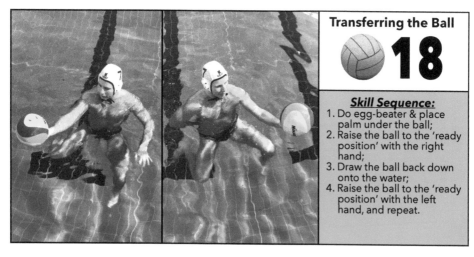

Transferring the Ball

18

Skill Sequence:
1. Do egg-beater & place palm under the ball;
2. Raise the ball to the 'ready position' with the right hand;
3. Draw the ball back down onto the water;
4. Raise the ball to the 'ready position' with the left hand, and repeat.

ANALYSIS OF DRIBBLING THE BALL

Head Up Freestyle
Perform head up freestyle and allow the ball to float in front of the face.

Speed & Vision
Dribbling becomes easier the faster a player swims, and try to look over the top of the ball to maximise vision.

The Ball
The arms may occasionally guide the ball, but the ball should ride along on the bow wave that is created by the head and face.

Dribbling the Ball

19

Skill Sequence:
1. Arms guide the ball, but don't knock or hit;
2. The ball moves ahead on the face 'bow' wave;
3. Keep head high, eyes looking over the ball;
4. High elbow recovery, arched back & use a strong kick.

'George French (CLU) plays in the Air Force vs Cal Lutheran match, score 14-8', by Chris Hunkeler, (2 Sep 2106). [See p.211].

19. Dribbling The Ball

The quickest way to move the ball around the water polo field is by passing, but if all players are closely marked it may be necessary to dribble the ball for a short distance.

This essential skill begins by doing head up freestyle and allowing the ball to float in front of the face. While swimming, the arms may occasionally guide the ball, but should not hit it as the ball essentially rides along on the bow wave that is created by the head and face. Dribbling becomes easier the faster a player swims. Remember to always try and look over the top of the ball to maximise vision.

Players should be ready to pick-up the ball and place it into the ready position before passing it off at the first opportunity. One last word of caution is to never dribble the ball too far, as it slows down the attack, it runs the 'shot clock' down, and gives the defense time to organise themselves.

20. Spinning With The Ball

Being able to quickly spin around in the water is another practical yet often overlooked skill that has many applications. During a game, a player often needs to turn quickly to shield the ball from an opponent, or they might gain a more advantageous scoring position by spinning away from a defender, so being able to quickly spin in a circle when required, is a very important skill.

However, the direction one spins in the water will depend on whether the player is right or left-handed. A left-hander should usually spin clockwise, whereas a right-hander should spin anti-clockwise, as spinning in the opposite direction is awkward. To quickly spin around in a circle while holding the ball, face the ball with the palm of the hand behind it. Drop and cross the legs, then brace them against the water and use the stomach muscles to create torque by unwinding like a corkscrew, which should be performed as fast as possible. To prevent the ball from flying away due to centrifugal forces, keep it nestled close to the face with your palm behind it, and keeping both elbows and arms lifted clear of the water will cut down on water resistance.

Summary

There are many other variations and adaptations of ball handling skills that can be programmed and performed, but the techniques outlined in this chapter are the most commonly used ball control skills for water polo players. After these skills have been introduced, practiced and

Spinning with the Ball

 20

Skill Sequence:
1. Face the ball with your palm behind;
2. Hold the ball close to the face, arms clear of the water;
3. Cross the legs over and brace;
4. Contract stomach muscles and unwind to build torque and speed;
5. Corkscrew away from a defender.

Experienced coaches know that 'perfect practice makes perfect'.

mastered, they form (along with passing and catching skills) the basis of most skills practices for water polo athletes. In the next chapter, new players will learn how to effectively pass and catch the ball under different situations.

Checklist of Ball Handling Skills

Skill #	Skill Name	✔	Date Mastered
14	Swimming with the Ball		
15	Balance with the Ball		
16	Ball Control		
17	Ball Pick Up		
a	*Under-ball Pick Up*		
b	*Roll-over & Pick Up*		
c	*Push-under & Pick Up*		
d	*Assisted Pick Up*		
18	Transferring the Ball		
19	Dribbling the Ball		
20	Spinning with the Ball		

Chapter 5
PASSING & CATCHING SKILLS

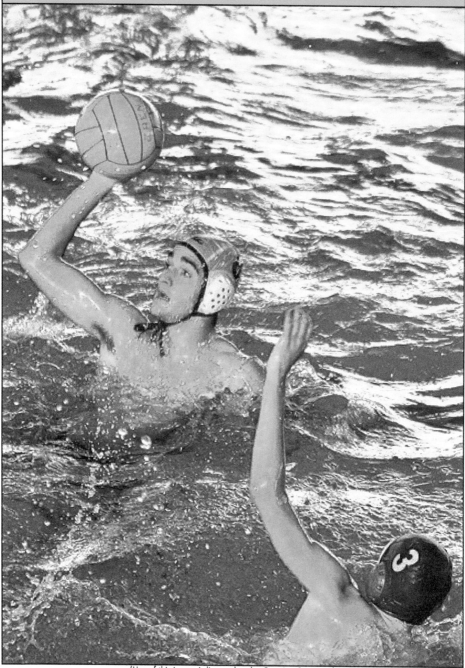

(Use of this image is licensed under Creative Commons).

PASSING & CATCHING SKILLS...

"Skill and confidence are an unconquered army."
George Herbert

Why Passing & Catching Skills Are Important

Acquiring passing and catching skills are core competencies for most invasion games and this is particularly so for playing water polo. However, the transfer of passing and catching skills learned on land, are not easily transferred to the water.

Whether passing to players swimming up for an attack or into the centre-forward, a number of critical aspects need to be considered when passing the ball. The following section examines a number of principles concerning what goes into developing good passes.

21. Principles of Passing & Catching

a. Preparation

With the speed of modern water polo, there is little time to think once you have received the ball and are preparing to make a pass. Therefore players need to think two steps ahead of their actual physical touch of the ball. Decide what you are going to do with the ball if and when it arrives.

If you don't know what you're going to do with the ball, immediately pass it to someone else who does.

b. Accuracy

The main consideration when passing is to always give accurate passes. Passes should generally be made to a teammates' throwing arm or onto the water. To successfully pass any higher up the pass needs to be directed to a specific hand. Try at all times to give passes that can't be contested by placing the ball at the furthest possible reach from any defenders.

c. Weight

The weight of a pass refers to how hard or soft it is thrown. Most beginners make the mistake of throwing very soft 'lob' style passes thinking this will assist their teammates to catch the ball. When in fact, a soft pass is actually harder to catch than a firmly thrown pass. A pass thrown firmly forces itself onto a catchers hand much better than a soft pass.

d. Trajectory

Unless intentionally throwing a lob, most water polo passes need to be thrown in a fairly flat trajectory, which both helps the passer control the throw and greatly assists

Pass & Catch Principles

21

Skill Sequence:
1. Preparation
2. Accuracy
3. Weight
4. Trajectory
5. Timing
6. Tempo
7. Communication
8. Conceal Intentions
9. Simple Passes
10. Chance & Opportunity
11. Always Attack

the catcher to absorb the impact of the pass. A high throw or lob is actually more difficult to juggle and catch.

e. Timing

An effective pass must be well-timed to arrive at its intended destination when it is needed. The pass should arrive not just before or just after it is called for, but exactly when it is required by the receiver.

f. Tempo

When in possession of the ball, all actions should be performed as quick as possible with the aim of out-maneuvering and confusing the defense. Passes that are moved around quickly stand a much better chance of confusing the defense.

g. Communication

Communication between the passer and an intended receiver must be very clear. Holding back a pass until the exact moment it is required is an attacking skill that can create many scoring opportunities. Communication with teammates can be verbal, or non-verbal in the form of a raised hand or a wink. Never pass the ball to teammates swimming with their head down or who aren't looking at you.

◀A pass should arrive, not just before or just after it is called for but, exactly when it is required by the receiver.

▶Players should look to pass the longest possible pass down-field first, then work backwards from that and make shorter passes to the side of the pool if down-field options aren't open (Pictured - 'Kyriakos Pontikeas, player for Olympiakos, Greece', by by Kallipon, (30 May 2016). [See p.211].).

If looking to catch the ball, raise your hand when you are open and ready to receive a pass, which tells your teammates they have passing options and also gives them a target for which to aim their pass.

h. Conceal Intentions

Defenders can often read the intentions of attackers and attempt interceptions, so sometimes disguise passes either by looking away or by looking in a completely different direction from where you actually intend passing the ball.

i. Simple Passes

The majority of passes in a game are basically designed to maintain possession. Beginners frequently overestimate their abilities, become impatient and often throw bad passes, when just keeping possession is a skill in itself. Throwing a successful defense splitting pass is like threading a needle and requires a great degree of skill. Most beginner and intermediate players should keep their passes simple at all times.

j. Chance & Opportunity

There are moments and situations in any game where passing through small gaps into tight spaces might result in a goal. Players should know that taking risks in the attacking third of the field can result in successes without too much risk. Conversely, a much more conservative approach needs to be taken when passing in the defensive third of the field.

k. Always Attack

Players should look to pass the longest possible pass down-field first, then work backwards from that and make shorter passes to the side of the pool if down-field options aren't open. The aim of a long pass is to launch the attack, switch the play or find a teammate in space. When players see a breaking player they should make the longest pass they can. A long pass is generally a better attacking option than a short pass, but this always depends on the situation.

All the above factors are important considerations when making passes to teammates. The following exercises and techniques detail how best to improve the efficiency and effectiveness of practicing for passing and catching drills.

22. Passing Balance

As basic as it sounds, a player must achieve height out of the water before a capable pass can be thrown. To do

Passing Balance

22

Skill Sequence:
1. Begin with egg-beater kick, lean slightly forward;
2. Scull with the non-throwing hand;
3. Keep shoulders & elbow clear of the water;
4. Vigorous leg action to lift the body higher.

this efficiently, begin by performing egg-beater kick with hips and legs kept high to elevate the shoulders clear of the water and in the process achieve a balanced position.

Players should lean slightly forward and scull with the non-throwing hand to establish a well balanced passing platform. The foot speed of the egg-beater kick should be increased to lift the body higher out of the water and the throwing arm is raised to the ready position. At this point the throwing elbow should be clear of the water and the player will be in the correct position to make pass or even receive a catch.

23. Pass Accuracy

Passing the ball effectively in any game is all about accuracy or 'hitting the target'. But what is the target? In water polo the ultimate aim is to throw the ball into the goal, so the goal becomes the target when we are shooting. But what about when we are just passing? During any game our passing 'target' constantly changes depending on where our teammates are and what they are doing. Passing safely (ie. keeping the ball away from the defense) becomes quite difficult as the passer is required to make a judgment about where and when they should send the ball. However, the player catching the ball can greatly assist by providing their teammates with a passing 'target'.

Players catching the ball can create a passing target by lightly splashing the water (for a wet pass), or by lifting their hand (for a dry pass). The spot being splashed or the hand in the air should indicate the exact position where your teammate prefers to receive the ball. During a game the situation is usually more intense, but the passer still needs to know that the catcher is looking at them and is ready to receive the ball. To assist further, the catcher should give some indication of where they want the ball either by splashing the water (for a wet pass), or lifting their hand to where they want the ball to arrive (for a dry pass).

Pass Accuracy

23

Skill Sequence:
1. Always pass to an incontestable safe space
2. The catcher can assist the passer by:
   - splashing the water lightly (for a wet pass)
   - holding their hand in the air (for a dry pass)

'Zac Polmanteer (Redlands) and Riley Smith (LMU) play in the Loyola Marymount vs Redlands match, score 12-11', by Chris Hunkeler, (2 Sep 2016). [See p. 211].

When passing to players who are swimming, try to place the ball so that it arrives at least 1m ahead of them and on the side away from any defenders. For teammates who are stationary, try to place the ball so that it arrives in a position where the defender virtually has to climb over your teammate to get to it. By doing this, you have automatically shielded the ball from the defender with your teammate.

24. The Wet Pass

This pass is known as a wet pass purely because it is passed onto the water and the ball becomes 'wet' in the process. This pass should be targeted onto the water about 1m in front of, but preferably on the throwing arm side of the recipient.

To perform a wet pass begin by performing egg-beater kick with hips and legs kept high, which should elevate the shoulders clear of the water. Leaning slightly forward and sculling with the non-throwing hand, increase foot speed of the egg-beater kick to raise the body higher, then raise the ball to the ready position. Keeping the elbow clear of the water the throw is performed forward of the shoulder using the forearm and the wrist, with a distinct snapping of the fingers. The ball should leave the hand spinning slightly backwards.

Skill Sequence:
1. A pass thrown onto the water usually to a swimmer.
2. Keep shoulders & elbow clear of the water
3. Pass from the forearm, wrist & finger snap
4. Pass onto the water 1m from the catcher
5. Pass to the side of their dominant hand

'Dayne Jagga (LMU) plays in the Loyola Marymount vs Redlands match, score 12-11', by Chris Hunkeler, (2 Sep 2016). [See p.211].

25. The Dry Pass

A dry pass is named by nature of the fact that it is not passed onto the water, instead the ball is thrown directly onto a teammates hand and caught 'dry'. This is more challenging as the pass must be targeted accurately onto the recipients hand at a point above their catching shoulder and at their eye-level or above.

Begin by performing egg-beater kick with hips and legs kept high, which should elevate the shoulders clear of the water. Leaning slightly forward and sculling with the non-throwing hand, increase foot speed of the egg-beater kick to raise the body higher in the water, then raise the

The Dry Pass

Skill Sequence:
1. Keep shoulders & elbow clear of the water
2. Pass from the forearm, wrist & finger snap
3. Pass to your teammates raised catching hand
4. Pass must be firm & flat (not soft or curved)

'Water polo player from LHS, USA looking to throw a dry pass', by Pexels, (2015). [See p. 211].

A BALANCED PASSING POSITION

Elbow Clear
The player is in the correct position to pass or receive the ball when the throwing elbow is clear of the water.

Body Position
Leaning slightly forward and sculling with the non-throwing hand to establish balance.

Egg Beater Kick
The foot speed of the egg-beater kick is increased to lift the body higher out of the water and the throwing arm is raised to the ready position.

Skill Sequence:
1. Point the catching hand towards the incoming ball;
2. Intensely watch the ball onto the hand;
3. Meet & cushion the ball out in front;
4. Catching fingers widely spaced & relaxed;
5. Absorb the force & allow the arm to continue backwards after contact.

ball to the ready position. Keeping the elbow clear of the water the throw is performed forward of the shoulder using the forearm and the wrist, with a distinct snapping of the fingers. As with the wet pass, the ball should leave the hand spinning slightly backwards.

To send a longer pass, regardless of whether it is intended to be caught wet or dry, the passer needs to use more of a forceful shooting action to successfully achieve the added distance.

26. Preferred Side Catch

To successfully catch a dry pass coming from the catchers preferred side, perform egg-beater kick with hips and legs kept high, which should elevate the shoulders clear of the water. Increase the foot speed of the egg-beater kick to lift the body higher in preparation for receiving the pass, and at the same time focus intensely on the incoming ball.

For a catch coming from the catchers preferred side, point your hand towards the incoming ball with fingers relaxed and widely spaced. Meet the ball out in front of the body, but cushion it into the palm as it arrives. The feel of the ball onto the fingertips is a critical component of the catch and is a skill that develops with more and more practice. Allow your wrist and elbow to absorb the full force of the throw until control has been gained. At this point you should once again be in the ready position to pass or shoot.

27. Non-Preferred Side Catch

Being able to catch a ball coming from a catchers' non-preferred side is a skill that is often either not taught well or not at all, but is essential to becoming a well-rounded water polo player. Classifying a pass as coming from either your preferred or non-preferred side will depend solely on whether you are right or left handed.

To successfully catch this pass, perform egg-beater kick with hips and legs kept high, which should elevate the shoulders clear of the water. Increase the foot speed of the egg-beater kick to lift the body higher in preparation for receiving the pass, and at the same time focus intensely on the incoming ball.

For a catch coming from the non-preferred side, the catcher should, be facing either the goal or a teammate with their shoulders square on, or parallel to the intended target. The catching hand is extended straight out in front of the body, just above the level of the water with the palm facing up. Intensely watch the ball as it arrives onto the palm and

Non-Preferred Side Catch

27

Skill Sequence:
1. Intensely watch the ball coming onto the hand from the non-preferred side;
2. Palm facing up & extended out in front;
3. Shoulders should be squared to where you will be sending the a pass or shot;
4. Catch & raise the ball to the 'ready' position.

ANALYSIS OF THE CATCH

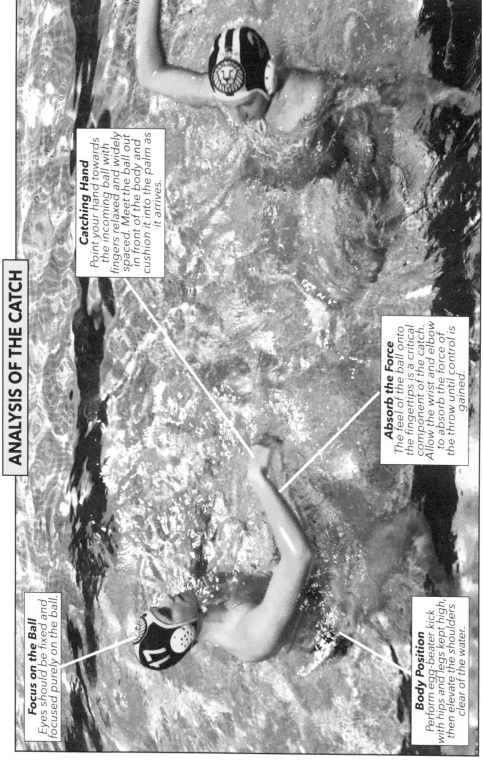

Catching Hand
Point your hand towards the incoming ball with fingers relaxed and widely spaced. Meet the ball out in front of the body and cushion it into the palm as it arrives.

Absorb the Force
The feel of the ball onto the fingertips is a critical component of the catch. Allow the wrist and elbow to absorb the force of the throw until control is gained.

Focus on the Ball
Eyes should be fixed and focused purely on the ball.

Body Position
Perform egg-beater kick with hips and legs kept high, then elevate the shoulders clear of the water.

Roll Over Pass

28

Skill Sequence:
1. Big breaststroke kick to create space;
2. Place your hand under the ball;
3. Roll over onto your back & look for the target;
4. Use egg-beater kick for lift, then pass.:
5. Pass around the arm of the defender.

'Water polo player about to perform a roll over pass', by jj_mom, (24 Sep 2013). [See p.211].

absorb the force of the throw onto the hand. The caught ball is then quickly brought around in an arc and lifted up into the ready position for another pass or shot.

In addition the normal passing action, the next four passing skills consist of specialist passes that can be used in various game situations where it may not be practical to use a conventional or straight forward pass.

28. Roll Over Pass

The roll-over pass is most often used to pass the ball to teammates when under pressure, and as such is one of the most vital passing skills that players can develop.

The simplest way to perform the roll over pass is to position the ball at arms length and perform a big breaststroke kick towards the ball. Then reach out and place your hand underneath the ball before rolling onto your back to find the passing target. As the body rolls over the wrist should remain in the same position underneath the ball. Finish off by increasing the egg-beater kick to raise the shoulders and throw with the elbow clear of the water.

29. Scoop Pass

The scoop pass can be used to pass around a defender, save time or to conceal the ball's intended target. This pass

Scoop Pass

29

Skill Sequence:
1. Keep shoulders & elbow clear of the water;
2. Place your hand under & behind the ball;
3. Effect the scoop throw from the shoulder joint;
4. Keep the elbow fixed throughout the throw;
5. Use a scoop when a pick up pass might be knocked down from behind.

can also be used as a very effective and powerful shot by increasing the speed and power of the throw. The passer should fully extend the arm and place their hand under the ball. Then increase egg-beater kick to raise the shoulders and elbow clear of the water. The elbow should be locked throughout as all the power for this pass comes from the shoulder. Rapidly contract the chest muscles and finish the throw off with a wrist flick.

30. Back Pass

The back pass can be used to quickly send a ball to a teammate that may be somewhere behind your position,

Back Pass

30

Skill Sequence:
1. Keep shoulders & elbow clear of the water;
2. Place hand under ball keeping elbow high;
3. Effect the backwards throw from the elbow joint;
4. Keep the elbow above the ball & flick the wrist to end.

and it is also an effective pass to conceal the ball's intended target. This throw can also be used as a very effective backhand shot by increasing both the speed and power.

The passer should increase their egg-beater kick to raise the shoulders and throwing elbow clear of the water. The hand is placed in front of and around the ball, but can also be wedged into the forearm if necessary. The elbow should be lifted high and then rapidly extended to effect the pass, which finishes with a strong wrist flick.

31. Push Pass

The push pass can be used to quickly send a ball straight ahead to a teammate without lifting the ball up to the ready position, and is most effective when there are trailing defenders prepared to knock down a raised arm. This throw can also be used as a very effective 'off the water' shot by increasing speed and power.

The passer uses their non-throwing arm for balance and increases egg-beater kick (or performs a breaststroke kick) to establish a firm platform, from which to impart the force needed for the throw. Bring the ball into the armpit and gently push it under the water and then release, before rapidly extending the shoulder and elbow forward. The key

Push Pass

31

**Skill Sequence:**
1. Keep shoulders & elbow clear of the water;
2. Spread fingers wide & grip the ball;
3. Throw from the armpit & extend the elbow;
4. Keep the elbow high throughout the push pass.

Skill Sequence:
1. Keep shoulders & elbow clear of the water;
2. Spread fingers wide & grip the ball;
3. Throw from the armpit & extend the elbow;
4. Keep the elbow high throughout the push pass.

point to performing a technically proficient push pass is to begin with the elbow high and maintain the elbow height throughout the entire throwing motion.

32. Pass & Catch Either Hand

Being 'ambidextrous' is the skill of being equally adept in the use of both left and right arms to pass or catch the ball, and this is a particularly useful skill for water polo players to acquire.

The ability to pass and catch with either hand undoubtedly increases a players level of skill, and being able to shoot and score goals with either hand can be a match winning advantage for any team. While learning to handle the water

▶This player is demonstrating the ideal location to catch a 'dry' pass. The ball should arrive on the wrist, in line with the top of the head, and just outside the shoulder line. 'Francesco Di Fulvio of Pro Recco, Italy', by Roberto Faccenda, (12 Nov, 2016). [See p. 211].

polo ball with either hand is not an easy task, ball handling drills involving both left and right hands should nevertheless be a constant component of every training session.

Summary

There are many other variations and adaptations of passing and catching that can be programmed and performed, but the techniques outlined in this chapter are the most commonly used passing and catching skills for water polo players. After these skills have been introduced, practiced and mastered, they form the basis for passing and catching skills for all water polo athletes. The focus of the next chapter will be to learn how to maintain possession of the water polo ball in different situations, when pressured and under challenging circumstances.

Skill #	Skill Name	✔	Date Mastered
21	Principles of Passing & Catching		
22	Passing Balance		
23	Pass Accuracy		
24	The Wet Pass		
25	The Dry Pass		
26	Preferred Side Catch		
27	Non-Preferred Side Catch		
28	Rollover Pass		
29	Scoop Pass		
30	Back Pass		
31	Push Pass		
32	Pass & Catch Either Hand		

Checklist of Passing & Catching Skills

Chapter 6
KEEPING POSSESSION

'Women's Water Polo team at practice [#054]', by Sean Fornelli, (2008). [See p. 211].

KEEPING POSSESSION....

"Take time to deliberate, but when the time for action has arrived, stop thinking and go in."
Napoleon Bonaparte

Why Keeping Possession Is Important

Scoring chances in any game of water polo don't arrive often, especially with a solid defense, the opposition goalkeeper and wayward shots accounting for most lost opportunities. But a common source of frustration particularly for beginners is an inability to maintain possession. Being able to effectively hold onto the ball is normally a function of how much experience a player has developed. Consequently, there are a number of phases in water polo where inexperienced players commonly get into difficulty. Mistakes that lead to a loss of possession are widespread, but identifying and minimising the most common causes will enhance your performance and the effectiveness of any team.

The problematic areas include: not maintaining personal possession of the ball particularly when being challenged; not passing with accuracy; not appropriately timing passes to teammates; not passing effectively when under pressure; and not using the entire water polo field to maximise possession.

Maintaining Possession

Possession is often lost due to the inexperience of new players who generally move slower, which tends to create opportunities for defenders to better contest and intercept the ball. Increasing the speed at which players swim, pick-up and pass the ball is a great first step in decreasing lost possession due to moving too slowly in the water.

A common misconception for most beginners is that it is not within the rules of water polo to play aggressively. In fact, players should be as aggressive as they need be in order to ward off determined opposition players from trying to intercept or strip the ball.

Being unaware of what is happening is another problematic area for beginners. For example, if an opponent is swimming at you from in front, you will need to sweep the ball around 180⁰ and create a shield with your body before they have any chance of interfering or stripping the ball away. Also shield the ball with your body if defenders are approaching from behind or the sides, making sure that egg-beater kick is working strongly and hips are high. The following skills and techniques detail how best to hold onto possession more effectively.

▶A team can't win if they don't have the ball. Losing possession can occur from: allowing yourself to be dispossessed; not passing accurately; not giving passes to teammates when required; not passing effectively when under pressure; committing an offensive foul; and not using the entire water polo field to maximise possession.

Shielding the Ball

33

Skill Sequence:
1. Shield and protect the ball with your body;
2. Maintain a 180° alignment drawn from the ball to the defender, with the ball holder in the centre;
3. Be mindful not to put the ball underwater;
4. Be aggressive in maintaining possession.

When in possession players should control the ball at arms length and take care not to bring the ball too close to their body, which may allow defenders to push the ball underwater, or harass any attempts to pass.

33. Shielding the Ball

Shielding is a basic and essential water polo skill and is best achieved by situating yourself between your opponent and the ball. Keep the ball at arms length with your back to the defender. Place yourself in the centre of an imaginary straight line, which runs from the ball, and is drawn through your head to the defender.

The defender will try to slide around either side of the person in possession, in an attempt to reduce the 180° straight line to a lesser angle approaching 90° or even less. But a diligent attacker should be able to maintain the 180° straight alignment, which should effectively shield the ball.

34. Timing a Pass

The main factor to consider with timing a pass correctly is that the pass must be thrown at the exact time that it is required by your teammate. Performing this skill successfully

MAINTAINING ALIGNMENT WHEN IN POSSESSION

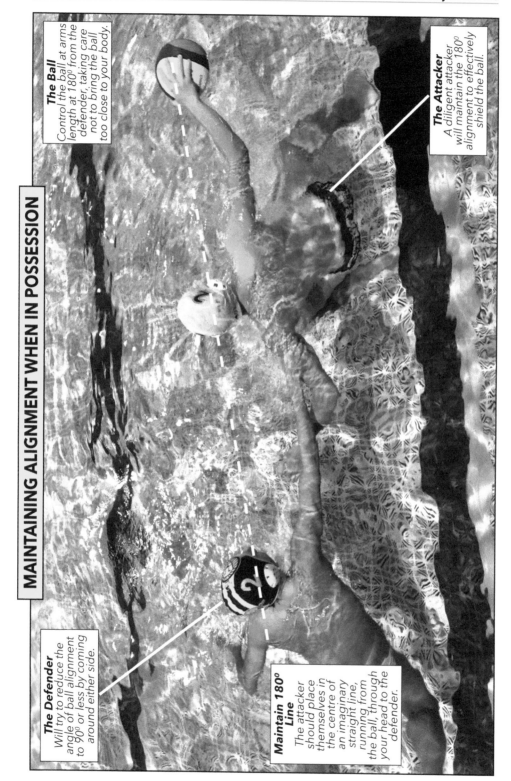

The Ball
Control the ball at arms length at 180⁰ from the defender, taking care not to bring the ball too close to your body.

The Attacker
A diligent attacker will maintain the 180⁰ alignment to effectively shield the ball.

The Defender
Will try to reduce the angle of ball alignment to 90⁰ or less by coming around either side.

Maintain 180⁰ Line
The attacker should place themselves in the centre of an imaginary straight line, running from the ball, through your head to the defender.

Timing a Pass

34

Skill Sequence:
1. Watch the receiver & be ready to send the pass;
2. Be careful not to pass too early or pass too late;
3. Send the pass, when the receiver requires it;
4. Leave 1m space when throwing 'wet' passes.

becomes more complicated if and when the pass needs to be thrown to a non-stationary, swimming or closely marked teammate, or also when time is running short.

Both practice and playing experience will develop an ability to judge when the optimal 'window' is open for a teammate to receive a pass. The pass needs to be withheld long enough so as to not arrive too early, but should be delivered before it is too late. Passes should be accurately thrown and arrive where and when teammates are best placed to receive them.

The passer must judge for themselves whether they have developed the ability to send the pass when and where it is required, and this skill only develops with a lot of practice and playing experience. It is important to remember that holding onto the ball is always more preferable to sending a bad pass, which can be contested, intercepted or mis-directed, and as a result hands the ball over to the opposition.

35. Passing Under Pressure

Being able to pass the ball to teammates when under pressure is another vital skill that attacking players must develop. The key point is that players need to shake off their defender and pass the ball at the exact moment it is required, without compromising on accuracy.

The simplest way to perform this skill is to swim the ball away from your opponent, then roll-over and pass. But this method can often be constrained by the available space at the side of the pool or other nearby defenders, so ensure you have the time and space required.

The 'T' Formation

Another effective skill for passing under pressure is known as the 'T' formation. To make a pass under pressure requires a strong egg-beater kick from the moment you receive the ball until the pass is effected. Players should initially shield the ball from their opponent. By turning the body through 90^0 away from their ball arm, drive the legs hard for support and make contact with the defenders chest using the non-throwing shoulder above the water. Most defenders will face square on, so also using your non-throwing forearm to make body contact below the water may assist with balance.

Then look to where you need to send the pass, judge whether you can throw that distance, and proceed if confident of success. Using the legs jump back away from your opponent and to the side while continuing to perform

Passing under Pressure

35

Skill Sequence:
1. Use strong egg-beater kick & lean slightly forward;
2. Breaststroke out and use the rollover pass;
3. Or, using a strong egg-beater kick, use the 'T-Formation';
4. Pass around (not through) the defender.

'Stephen Siri drives the ball to Matt Burton around Air Force defense, by Neon Tommy, (1 Dec 2012). [See p.211].

THE 'T' FORMATION

Keep Ball At Arms Length
Shield the ball at arms length from your opponent.

Egg Beater Kick
The T-Formation requires a strong egg-beater kick from the moment you receive until you pass the ball.

Prepare to Pass
Look to where you need to send the pass, judge whether you can throw that distance, and proceed if confident of success.

Shoulder Contact
Make contact with the defenders chest (who should be facing square on) using your non-throwing shoulder (above the water) and your non-throwing forearm (below the water).

strong egg-beater kick. Complete the skill by passing around the defender, not through or over their head. Be careful not to push the defender away with your non-throwing hand as this will incur a turnover foul for pushing off.

36. Drawing A Free Throw

While passing under pressure is an essential skill to develop, passing is of course made much easier and is much more accurate when not under pressure. Intentionally drawing a foul is an excellent method of temporarily relieving the pressure of a harassing defender and efforts to do so are often rewarded with a free throw.

Drawing a free throw is a common practice in water polo with both perimeter players and centre-forwards often attempting to draw fouls as part of their offensive strategy. This tactic is frequently used by skilled players, allowing them time to deliver an accurate and well-timed pass free of harassment. The real skill in gaining a free throw is not only knowing how, but exactly when to perform this tactical manoeuvre. To encourage a defender to commit a foul and hand you a free throw, simply take your hand off the ball when being challenged or tackled. You don't have to fake being sunk or lift your arm high into the air, just

Drawing a 'Free Throw'

36

Skill Sequence:
1. Protect & shield the ball with your body;
2. Confuse the defender by rolling your hand continually on & off the ball;
3. Take your hand off the ball when challenged;
4. If necessary, repeat until the foul is called;
5. Sit up and take your 'free throw', or shot (if within the 5m zone).

calmly elevate your hand slightly free of the ball while the defenders hand or arms are on you.

Although attackers may be in possession when shielding the ball, they are not technically holding the ball at that moment, so being 'grabbed, sunk, pulled back or impeded' should be sufficient grounds for the referee to award a free throw.

Good ball control and frequently rolling and lifting your hands on and off the ball while maintaining possession is an important skill for players to master if they are to perfect the tactical skill of drawing a free throw.

Using The Width Of The Pool

Another important factor for players in the offensive phase is to use as much of the pool as possible. Too many beginners restrict their movements to the centre of the field and often find themselves being backed up against other opponents when they actually have plenty of room to

Practice sessions are far more effective when all athletes are engaged, as shown in this image where there are enough practice balls for each athlete.

The attacking team should use as much pool width as possible, otherwise the defense gains an advantage as the working space of an attacking team is restricted. 'Greece vs Hungary Water Polo match at the World Junior Championship, Naples, Italy, 2004', by Massimo Finizio, (2004). [See p. 211].

manoeuvre. The defensive team gains a distinct advantage when the working space of the attacking team is restricted. Therefore, offensive teams should try to counteract this potential problem by actively trying to open up the full length and width of the water polo field.

Although the situation is constantly changing, knowing where you are in the field of play at any given time is a skill which comes with practice and match play, but beginners should be instructed to take advantage of the full dimensions of the water polo field whenever possible.

Summary

There are many other skills and techniques associated with keeping possession that can be practised and performed, but the techniques outlined in this chapter are those most commonly used for water polo players to hold onto possession. After these skills have been introduced, practiced and mastered, they form the basis of the skills necessary for maintaining possession for all water polo athletes.

The focus of the next chapter is to learn both the theory and skills necessary to effectively limit the scoring opportunities of a water polo team on the offensive.

Checklist of Possession Keeping Skills			
Skill #	Skill Name	✔	Date Mastered
33	Shielding the Ball		
34	Timing a Pass		
35	Passing Under Pressure		
36	Drawing a 'Free Throw'		

Chapter 7
DEFENSIVE SKILLS

'Concentrate on the ball when blocking. Rio de Janeiro - Seleção masculina brasileira de polo aquático vence a da Sérvia por 6 a 5 nos Jogos Olímpicos Rio 2016, no Parque Aquático Maria Lenk', by Fernando Frazão/Agência Brasil, Agência Brasil Fotografias, (10 Aug 2016). [See p. 211].

DEFENSIVE SKILLS...

"The most effective defense is, to block the offense as close as possible to their point of departure."
John Cotterill

Why Defensive Skills Are Important

As mentioned previously, there are some general principles of invasion games that can be applied to playing the game of water polo. Players participating in invasion games frequently alternate from taking on an offensive or defensive role depending upon whether their team is in possession of the ball at any given moment. The team in possession of the ball is commonly known as the 'offensive' or attacking team whereas the team not in possession of the ball is known as the 'defensive' or defending team.

Defense requires 'reactive' involvement, and is generally more passive than being actively on the attack. However, a solid defense is the backbone of any great team and will contribute to many victories.

The General Role Of Defense

The main role of a water polo defender is to always 'deny the shot', the objective being to stop opposing players from shooting and possibly scoring. Defenders should place themselves between any attacking players they are marking and their goal. They should closely monitor any 'threatening' opposition players who may be in their immediate area, and quickly close down any 'open space' that an attacking player is occupying. The term to 'guard or mark closely' in water polo should be interpreted as being very close, even body against body. No water polo defender is capable of moving fast enough through 1m or 2m of water to close down an imminent shooter.

Defenders should also attempt to intercept passes, block any shots and make tackles on attacking players in possession of the ball, sometimes as a last line of defense. Defenders need to develop an ability to 'read the game' so as to anticipate movements and block potential incoming threats, before it's too late.

Defenders must balance the need to deal with an imminent attacking threat against the need to maintain their balanced defensive position. An ability to time defensive interventions to occur at exactly the required moment is another important defensive skill. Defenders should also be aware of the tactical interpretations of the rules, which allow the intentional 'fouling' of an attacking player to prevent shots at the goal.

A solid defense is the backbone of any great team and will contribute to many victories. 'Water Polo By The Sea' at Bondi, Australia, 2012.

Defenders in general should be careful not to give away water space to attacking players too easily and this is particularly important after losing the swim off or when defending at the re-start after a goal. Always try to make the down field progress of the offensive team a difficult passage.

The Roles Of Defense

The tasks of a defender in any water polo game are numerous, but success is achieved when each and every player limits their own individual mistakes. In general terms, one can't go too wrong by adhering to the following defensive duties:

- *Know what your position is, in the field*
- *Be aware of where the ball and attackers are*
- *Listen for instructions from the coach*
- *Communicate with your goalkeeper*
- *Communicate with your defensive teammates*
- *Always situate yourself between an attacker and your goal*
- *Anticipate any potential incoming threats*
- *Attempt to intercept opposition passes*
- *Close down any space around attackers*
- *Closely guard any 'threatening' players*
- *Tackle opposing players in possession of the ball*
- *Stop attacking players from shooting*
- *Explode into counter-attack on a turnover*
- *Send the ball away from your goal area*

Roles For Defensive Positions

It's important to remember that when a team is defending, there are normally no set positions as any one defender can be called upon to mark any one attacker, anywhere, at any time. However, at the point of a turnover, the following would be the roles of designated players, at least in the initial part of the defensive phase.

a. Forwards

When a team loses possession and rotates into the defensive phase, it is the job of those up front to quickly attach themselves to the closest opposition players to prevent the ball being passed down field. They should never allow attackers to swim past them, but once the ball has progressed down field, they should swim back into their half of the field and harass the opposition where possible. They should remain at the ready to explode into counter-attack when the time arrives.

b. The Halves/Drivers

Players in mid-field such as halves, should be heading back to support the defense and assist the backs around the goal area immediately possession has been lost. They should be aware to cut off any counter-attacks and cover breaking players or intercept any long passes as they are retreating.

c. The Backs

Players in the back line should immediately look to balance their position, call for assistance from the halves and forwards, and check with the goalkeeper on where they may want them to position. They now become the defensive back-line and must not allow attackers to penetrate beyond them. They should mark their opposition players very tightly, foul if required and deny all attempted shots on goal.

A centre-back should also try to unbalance the attack by using strong egg-beater kick to push the centre-forward to

▶A centre-back should try to unbalance the attack by pushing the centre-forward to the side or out past 4m or 5m from the goal, which will make any shots much less effective. 'Edward Moss (LMU) and Luke Ritter (LB) play in the Long Beach State vs Loyola Marymount match, score 11-7', by Chris Hunkeler, (undated). [See p. 211].

the side or out past 4m or 5m from the goal, which will make any shots much less effective.

d. Goalkeeper

Being located on the goal line, the goalkeeper has the most important defensive role in any team. It is their responsibility to block all shots on goal, and communicate with and assemble the team's defenses. The individual and specialised role of the goalkeeper is covered in much more detail in Chapter 10.

'Reading' The Game

Developing an understanding of how a player fits into a game, and what they are expected to do is a gradual process that develops with practice and experience. But being able to 'read the game' and 'communicate' are two important factors that can accelerate the development of defensive skills.

Players should try to 'read the game' when on defense, to understand what their position is in the field, where the ball is, and anticipate what is most likely to occur next. They should also be aware of where the opposing players are, and be able to anticipate any potential incoming threats. Defenders can be greatly assisted in being able to read the game by communicating with their goalkeeper and other defensive teammates, while at the same time listening out

◄A goalkeeper should never take their eyes off the ball as a shot can come from anywhere in the field at anytime. 'Frame extracted from miniDV movie taken May 2005 at a boys high school water polo match', by Ryanjo, (16 Apr 2006). [See p. 211].

Principles of Defense

 37

Knowledge:
1. **Delay** - do everything possible to slow down the offense;
2. **Support** - support your teammates & restrict space;
3. **Concentrate** the defense - this resticts the available attacking space;
4. **Balance** - defense should be evenly balanced in a defensive shape
5. **Discipline** - must remain disciplined, patient, practice restraint & stick to the plan.

'Lee Griffin (LB) and Jon Beck (LMU) play in the Long Beach State vs Loyola Marymount match, score 11-7', by Chris Hunkeler, (2 Sep 2016). [See p.211].

for instructions from their coach. Specific knowledge and skills applicable for defenders are:

37. Principles Of Defense

There are a number of guiding principles that can help to effect a solid and consistent defense both for teams and individuals, and these are:

a. Delay

After losing possession of the ball the defending team should do everything possible to slow down the offense or prevent a quick counter-attack. This can be accomplished by defenders reducing the time and space of the ball carriers, applying pressure, using feints and lunges, and in this way they can delay the ball being moved down field. Defenders should concentrate on what attacking players are doing and where they're going, as opposed to the ball. They should try to pressure ball carriers to alter course away from the goal by forcing them to turn away or pass. Delaying tactics can also be accomplished on a team basis by conceding expendable areas of the pool and bringing defenders back to occupy the more dangerous attacking areas in front of goal.

b. Support & Close Up

Remembering that the offensive team are trying to create space, an important goal for the defense is to try to close up any space, support each other and concentrate in the defensive half of the field. Defenders should be prepared to leave outside and wing attackers to focus on drivers swimming into the much more 'dangerous' goal area. By doing this the defense also compacts the goal area, which will force long distance shots.

c. Concentrate The Defense

If a defending team is unsure of its capabilities, defenders should give away space in less dangerous parts of the field and fall back to cover the central goal area when and where possible. As the working space of an attacking team is restricted by the concentrated defense, the more the defending team gains the advantage. Individual defenders should then prevent penetration through their compacted defense and deny the offense from swimming into and around the attacking zone.

d. Balance

If the swimming mobility of the offensive team is being used to upset a defense, then maintaining balance is critical to counter the attacking drives. In water polo, defensive balance is maintained by the 'switching' of defenders according to which attacking players are most 'dangerous'. Defenders should be evenly spread to balance and retain the defensive shape.

e. Discipline

When a defending team has observed the previous four defensive principles, it will find itself in good order to deal

A BALANCED DEFENSE

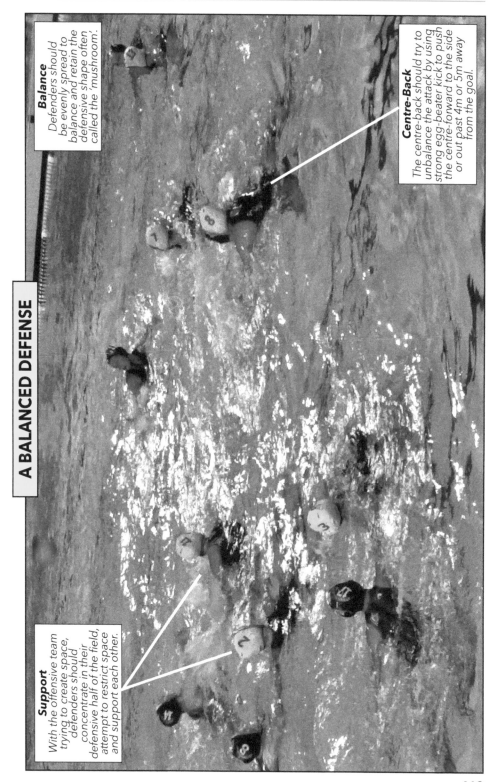

Balance
Defenders should be evenly spread to balance and retain the defensive shape often called the 'mushroom'.

Centre-Back
The centre-back should try to unbalance the attack by using strong egg-beater kick to push the centre-forward to the side or out past 4m or 5m away from the goal.

Support
With the offensive team trying to create space, defenders should concentrate in their defensive half of the field, attempt to restrict space and support each other.

with most offensive contingencies. However, defenders need to remain disciplined and patient, exercise control, practice restraint, stick to the plan and not be reckless or take any risks in defense.

Defenders should understand that their role is to react to and anticipate offensive actions, and that principles of defense are dynamic and constantly evolve according to the developments of each game. With each ball that is passed, or whenever an attacker swims into a new position the tactics of the defense may need to change a little or may alter drastically.

38. Guarding or Marking

The individual skill of guarding or marking an opponent is much different in water polo when compared with other invasion games. The main difference being that water polo is obviously played in the water, which naturally slows down one's ability to make a quick response. In order to adapt to the constraining nature of playing a game in water, defenders should position themselves very close to their opponents. In fact, the closer the better and most coaches recommend direct body to body contact. Inexperienced players may find this concept difficult to grasp, but effective tackling and

Guarding or Marking

38

Skill Sequence:
1. Set yourself between the attacker & your goal
2. Place your chest against their back;
3. For RH - look over their left shoulder; LH - over the right shoulder;
4. Vigorous egg-beater kick with hips up;
5. Show the referee your hands - no fouling;
6. Be higher in the water than your opponent.

Tackling

39

Skill Sequence:
1. Wait until the opponent is in contact with the ball;
2. As they turn, use egg-beater kick to lunge;
3. Place your hand on their chest to balance;
4. Mirror your arm with their passing arm;
5. Reach ahead to try & knock the ball away.

The perfect tackle to stop a pass or shot. 'Iran men's national water polo team [#1]', by Ansari, (2016). [See p. 211].

blocking of shots requires that the defender is always close enough to make contact with the attackers throwing arm.

The other slightly different thing for defenders to focus on is to watch the attacker, rather than the ball. By concentrating solely on the ball, a water polo defender runs the risk of losing track of their moving attacker, which may result in a quick pass and goal to an unguarded player. So when on defense, players should concentrate on marking their opponents rather than being too concerned about where the ball is located. After all, if all the attackers are guarded, the ball can't throw itself!

39. Tackling

A defender should always place themselves between their opponent and their goal, which means that in order to shield the ball most attackers will turn their back to the goal they are attacking.

Therefore defenders should guard their opponent by placing their chest against their opponents back, and if possible on the opposite shoulder to the attackers throwing arm. Defenders should guard a right hander by looking over their left shoulder, and a left hander by looking over their right shoulder. This is because a right handed forward will

ANALYSIS OF THE TACKLE

The Tackle
Tackle or foul the attacker as they receive the pass by using a breaststroke leg action to lunge forward and block the ball.

Positioning
Defenders should place their chest against their opponents back, looking over the opposite shoulder to their throwing arm.

Preparation
Increase foot speed to raise the hips and gain height out of the water, then raise up above the opponent and challenge.

normally roll out to the left to attempt a shot, and vice-versa for a left hander.

To effect a tackle, increase foot speed to raise the hips and gain height out of the water, then raise up above the opponent to make the challenge. Time the tackle and foul the attacker as they receive the pass by using a breaststroke leg action to lunge forward and block the ball. Defenders in the hole should always attempt to foul the centre-forward in order to prevent them from shooting.

40. Fouling

For most players new to the game, committing a foul might seem like a negative thing to do, but fouling is an often used water polo tactic for any team on defense. The rules state that after being fouled, an attacker must pass to a teammate before a shot can be taken (unless outside 5m). Therefore, once fouled inside 5m, an attacking player can longer shoot directly at goal and is required to pass the ball to a teammate. This means that a talented forward can be prevented from shooting and an attack nullified simply by the use of intelligent fouling.

To effectively use this tactic, defenders should know when, and when not to foul as the situation is always changing,

Fouling

40

Skill Sequence:
1. Stay in very close contact with your opponent;
2. Know when & when not to foul;
3. Not fouling runs the 'shot clock' down faster;
4. Once the foul is awarded, contest the free throw from 1m away;
5. Always foul the centre-forward to stop any shots.

and not fouling can run down the attacking teams' shot clock much quicker. To foul a player, try to coincide your tackle with the arrival of the ball and reach over their shoulder to knock the ball away. If they roll onto their back to pass, lunge forward with a big breaststroke kick and place one hand on their chest then try to block the pass or knock the ball away.

Once the foul has been given, the defender can use one arm to block from where the foul occurred, but they must otherwise allow the free throw to be taken. Remember that in water polo, a foul stops the game clock until the free throw is taken, which can lengthen a game considerably.

Defenders should be familiar with fouling in and outside the 5m area, and should be very careful not to foul a good attacker just outside this zone, as they are then permitted to take a quick free shot at the goal.

41. Blocking Passes & Interceptions

Another often effective defensive tactic is to use an arm to block an attackers pass. The key to effective blocking is to get as close to the attacker as possible then mirror their throwing arm with your blocking arm. As the attacker and defender usually face each other, in effect a right-handed attacker should be blocked with the defenders left arm and vice-versa.

Blocking & Interceptions

41

Skill Sequence:
1. Stay low in the water with hips up;
2. Use an explosive breaststroke kick for lift;
3. Perform a vertical jump as ball comes near.
4. The blocking arm must reflect the throwing arm;
5. Lean forward into the shooter;
5. Intensely focus on the ball (hint - look for the brand).

'Ilija Mustur - Montpellier Water Polo, France', by Roikiine, (20 Feb 2013). [See p. 211].

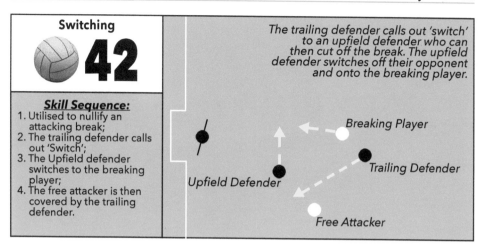

Switching

42

Skill Sequence:
1. Utilised to nullify an attacking break;
2. The trailing defender calls out 'Switch';
3. The Upfield defender switches to the breaking player;
4. The free attacker is then covered by the trailing defender.

The trailing defender calls out 'switch' to an upfield defender who can then cut off the break. The upfield defender switches off their opponent and onto the breaking player.

Breaking Player

Trailing Defender

Upfield Defender

Free Attacker

The defender should completely concentrate on the ball in order to have a better chance of blocking a pass. The defender should also be careful not to use two hands to effect the block as this will incur a major foul and result in a 5m penalty shot.

42. Switching

Another useful defensive skill is 'switching', which occurs when two defenders effectively exchange the attacking players they are guarding. This situation can occur when players on the attacking team may have perhaps out-swum a defender and a 'break' has been achieved. In this event, switching is best utilised as a defensive tactic to nullify any break that might have been achieved by the attack. The trailing defender calls out 'switch' to an upfield defender who then cuts off the break. The upfield defender switches off their opponent and onto the breaking player. This manouevre can give the trailing defender time to catch up and switch onto the open attacker, who had been left free by the switching defender.

43. Blocking Shots

Another common defensive role is to block attempted shots at goal. To effect a block using one arm, rapidly

Blocking Shots

43

Skill Sequence:
1. Get as close to the shooter as possible;
2. Mirror their throwing arm with your blocking arm;
3. Use LH to block a RH shot & vice versa;
4. Concentrate intensely on the ball;
5. Never use two hands when blocking, especially within the 5m area.

'Matteo Morelli (USC) and Royce Daniel Laverne (CBU) play in the USC vs California Baptist match, score 16-3', by Chris Hunkeler, (2 Sep 2016). [See p.211].

increase the foot speed of your egg-beater kick to elevate yourself out of the water. Then raise the arm that mirrors the attackers throwing arm and focus intensely on the ball (looking for the brand mark) when attempting to block a shot. Interceptions should be attempted whenever and wherever possible and are an extension of the jumping skill (#13).

An effective defense against outside shooters is for members of the defense to raise their arms, effectively forming additional barriers and cutting down angles, which will also assist the goalkeeper.

◄Defenders should always try to make the down field progress of the offensive team a difficult passage. 'A spirited girls' high school water polo game in Central Florida in 2004', by Ryanjo, (posted 12 Apr 2006). [See p. 211].

44. Common Defensive Errors

Beginners and inexperienced players need to be aware of possible errors that members of a defense can unknowingly commit. Common mistakes that players can make when on defense include:

- *allowing an attacker to swim or jostle past you, which presents them with inside water and a scoring opportunity;*
- *solely focusing on the ball, which allows an attacker to swim away and be open for a pass;*
- *swimming out to confront an attacker, which allows a possible pass over the defenders head to a more dangerous attacker behind and closer to goal;*
- *helping a defensive teammate (ie. two defenders guarding one attacker), which will open up another attacker;*
- *not using strong egg-beater kick to lift yourself out of the water, which allows attackers to dominate;*
- *not fouling the centre-forward inside the 5m zone, when they receive the ball, which presents good centre-forwards with easy scoring opportunities; and...*
- *not listening to instructions from the coach or the goalkeeper, which can result in an unbalanced defense.*

Defend The Danger

Defenders should understand that their most important role is to defend what is most dangerous. Any attacking

Common Defensive Errors

44

Knowledge:
1. When on the defensive phase, players need to be aware of the most common errors that members of any defense can unknowingly commit.

◄Starts, re-starts and set plays can be vulnerable phases of a water polo game where the defensive team must be prepared to guard against pre-planned offensive tactics.

player moving inside the 5m mark must always be guarded closely by a defender. Watching attackers can be more important than watching the ball as the most dangerous attacking players can move quickly. At one moment it might be the player who slips in close to goal even when the ball is out at the 8m line. Or in the next moment it could be the unmarked attacker swimming across the 5m area ready to receive a pass across the goal. Defenders need to merge awareness with judgment and anticipate what is about to happen as well as guard against other possible eventualities.

Defending from Starts & Re-Starts

Starts, re-starts and set plays can be vulnerable phases of a water polo game where the offensive team may position attacking players to execute a pre-planned manoeuvre. An effective defense should be prepared for such possibilities by developing defensive tactics right from the swim off. Generally, all players on the defensive team need to quickly 'glue' themselves onto an opponent after:

- *a swim off has been lost*
- *a goal has been scored and there is a restart*
- *a neutral throw has been lost*
- *a corner throw is awarded to the offense*
- *a time-out expires*

In all of the above starts and restarts, defensive players should know what tactic is being used, who they are guarding and what their individual role entails. Best way of doing this is for each defender to commuunicate to each other the cap number of the player they will be guarding.

Summary

There are many other skills and techniques that can be programmed and performed in relation to effecting a solid

▶*Defenders should guard their opponent on the opposite shoulder to the attackers throwing arm. Guard a right handed attacker by looking over their left shoulder, and a left hander by looking over their right shoulder. This is because a right handed forward will normally roll out to the left to attempt a shot, and vice-versa for a left hander.*

water polo defense, but the techniques outlined in this chapter are those most commonly used by players in the defensive phase.

After these skills have been introduced, practiced and mastered, they form the basis of defensive skills for all water polo athletes. The focus of the next chapter will be to learn how offensive skills can be best used effectively to increase scoring opportunities of a water polo team against a determined defense.

Checklist of Defensive Skills

Skill #	Skill Name	✔	Date Mastered
37	Principles of Defense		
38	Guarding or Marking		
39	Tackling		
40	Fouling		
41	Blocking Passes & Interceptions		
42	Switching		
43	Blocking Shots		
44	Common Defensive Errors		

Chapter 8
OFFENSIVE SKILLS

'U.S. Navy, Marine Corps and Army service members play water polo at Mina Salman Pier', by Mike Lenart, (July 03, 2013). [See p.211].

"Nobody ever successfully defended anything, there is only attack and attack and attack..."
Gen. George S. Patton

Why Offensive Skills Are Important

A team going into an offensive phase usually gains the ball from their goalkeeper following a shot, from a goal throw, or perhaps in mid-field from an interception. But an offensive team can't usually score from their half of the field. To get the ball into the goal they need to move the ball forward, which requires that they penetrate into their attacking end of the field.

Offense requires 'active' involvement and so attackers must move at every opportunity. The aim for every team is to shoot the ball at the goal if and when possible, but a well defended goal will attempt to repel most shots from outside or long distance range. The attacking team should therefore attempt to break up the defense and move the ball closer to the goal, which can be achieved by passing and dribbling the ball forward. Attackers will achieve this more effectively if they open themselves up by swimming away from defenders.

To effectively move forward and get closer to goal an attacking team need to break up or unbalance the defense. Moving forward by dribbling the ball is a limited option, but passing the ball forward has much greater potential to disrupt the defense and exploit any resulting opportunities.

The General Role Of Attack

The simplified role of players on offense is to score goals where possible, and the next chapter will explore and is devoted solely to shooting techniques. But the effective spoiling tactics of a firm defense will, more often than not, require a more strategic approach to organising an attack.

If an attacking player is not able to shoot, pass, dribble or penetrate, they should still try to maintain possession and call for support, which is the next most important function of an attack. Players on the offensive team need to help and support their teammates who may be temporarily locked up or unable to pass. In this role attackers should help players in trouble so that the ball is kept moving and the attack maintains momentum.

The spoiling tactics of a firm defense will often require a strategic approach to organising an attack. 'A men's water polo exhibition game between the Pacific Tigers and Santa Clara Broncos at the Sullivan Aquatic Center in Santa Clara, California', by BrokenSphere, (18 July 2010). [See p.211].

◄One role of the drivers or halves is to be the passing link between the goalkeeper and backs, the wings, the forwards and centre-forward. 'Water Polo sprint for the ball at the 2012 Summer Olympics', by Adam Russell, (2 Aug 2012). [See p. 211].

To provide support, attackers need to spread themselves wide, and occupy space where they are in an open position to receive a pass, then communicate and help out other members of their team. Finally, even while throwing everything into the attack, the offensive team should keep an eye on defenders who may be preparing for a counter-attack, especially when the 'shot clock' is nearing its limit.

The Roles of Attack

Offensive players are normally designated as forwards or drivers (goal shooters), with the strongest player usually being placed in the centre-forward or 'hole' position. Some teams designate halves whose main job is to receive the ball from the goalkeeper or backs and send it on to the forwards or centre-forward, before joining in the attack. Specific roles for attacking players are:

a. Goalkeeper

Although a goalkeepers' main role is to stop shots on goal, they also play a significant offensive role in frequently launching the counter-attack. An ability to make long accurate and safe passes is critical to an effective counter-attack. The individual and specialised role of the goalkeeper is covered in much more detail in Chapter 10.

b. The Backs

After the transition from defense to offense has taken place, backs should break away from any opposition players and swim into open space, ready to receive a pass from the goalkeeper. After passing on to the halves or forwards, the backs should swim up to support the attack, but should always be prepared to resist and defend against turnovers.

c. The Halves (or Drivers)

Players in mid-field such as halves or drivers, should anticipate and launch counter-attacks immediately the ball is regained, by breaking away to support the offensive effort around the goal area. Their role is to be the passing link between the goalkeeper and backs, the wings, forwards and centre-forward. Once the ball is in the offensive third of the field, the halves should swim up to support the attack and shoot if and when the opportunity arises.

The strength, ability and experience of the centre-forward in struggling to get shots away while under great pressure, is one of the exciting features of water polo.

d. The Forwards (or Wings)

When a team gains possession and rotates into an offensive phase, it is the job of the forwards to detach themselves from their closest opposition players and to open themselves up to receive passes. They should also attempt to swim past the defenders to gain 'inside water', thereby positioning themselves between the defender and the goal if possible. Their role is also to pass into, and receive passes from the centre-forward, who often controls the attack. Balls sent into the centre-forward should generally be 'wet' passes. The forwards should be amongst the most potent and accurate shooters in the team and will try to play and shoot from their preferred side of the field according to whether they are left or right handed.

e. The Centre-Forward

The centre-forward or 'hole' is often the strongest and perhaps best shooter on a team, and they also often control the attack. Their strength, ability and experience in getting shots away while under pressure is one of the exciting features of water polo.

The centre-forward should attempt to occupy a position as close to the middle of goal as possible (but not inside the 2m zone), facing away from the goalkeeper, and push back against any resistance from the centre-back. The hole man needs to vigorously perform egg-beater kick to elevate the hips and shoulders, which will allow the use of their arms to shoot when an opportunity arises.

Watch The Defense

Developing an understanding of how a player fits into a game and what they are expected to do is a gradual process that develops with practice and experience. Being able to 'read the game' and 'communicate' are two important factors that can accelerate the development of offensive skills.

THE CENTRE-FORWARD

Shooting Ability
The centre-forwards ability and experience in getting shots away while under pressure is one of the exciting features of water polo.

Strength & Power
The centre-forward or 'hole-man' is often the strongest player on a team, and often controls the attack.

Draws in the Defense
A powerful centre-forward will draw in the defense, which opens up other attacking options.

'MNE vs CRO on 2010 Men's European Water Polo Championship in Zagreb', byEx13, (2010). [See p.211].

137

Principles of Attack

45

Knowledge:
1. **Counter-attack** - always counter-attack on gaining possession;
2. **Penetration** - swim into open space;
3. **Support** - make yourself open to receive passes;
4. **Mobility** - drive into open areas of the field;
5. **Width & Balance** - one defender should not be guarding two attackers;
6. **Creativity** - develop creativity and innovation in attack.

'Womens Water Polo at the World Swimming Championships, Melbourne 2007 [#1]', by Flying Cloud, (2007). [See p. 211].

Attacking players should develop their ability to 'read the game' to know and understand what their position is in the field and where the ball is. They should also be aware of where the defending players are and be able to anticipate any potential opportunities or threats.

Attacking players can be greatly assisted in 'reading the game' when they communicate with their teammates, while at the same time listening for instructions from their coach. Specific knowledge and skills for attackers can be classified as the 'principles of attack'.

45. Principles Of Attack

While the defense will no doubt do everything it can to intercept the ball or slow down any forward progress, there are a number of guiding principles that can contribute to mounting an effective water polo attack.

The transition from being on defense to going into an attacking phase occurs very quickly, and can often be anticipated. A defender who anticipates these transitions can gain a considerable advantage when breaking away on an offensive counter-attack.

a. Counter-Attack

A standard principle for any team transitioning into an attacking phase is to always counter-attack and move the ball upfield as soon as possible. In this way, quick goals can be scored by throwing long passes to breaking players. Breaking players should aim for a one-on-none, or two-on-one advantage, but should always be conscious of leaving a numerical disadvantage behind them in the event of a turnover.

b. Penetration

If the counter-attack is not successful or if it breaks down, a more static offensive play will need to be established. The kind of offensive play used will depend on a number of factors including: the skills of the players in the water (eg. centre-forward); the tactics of the defense; and even the score or what stage the game is at. Penetrating the defense can be achieved by swimming into space and passing to players who are open upfield. Attackers should always try to give safe passes that can't be contested.

c. Support

If an attacking player with the ball cannot score they will require support from other teammates around them, creating options to pass the ball, forwards, sideways or

◀Penetrating the defense can be achieved by passing to players who are open upfield, and driving into open space.

PRINCIPLES OF ATTACK

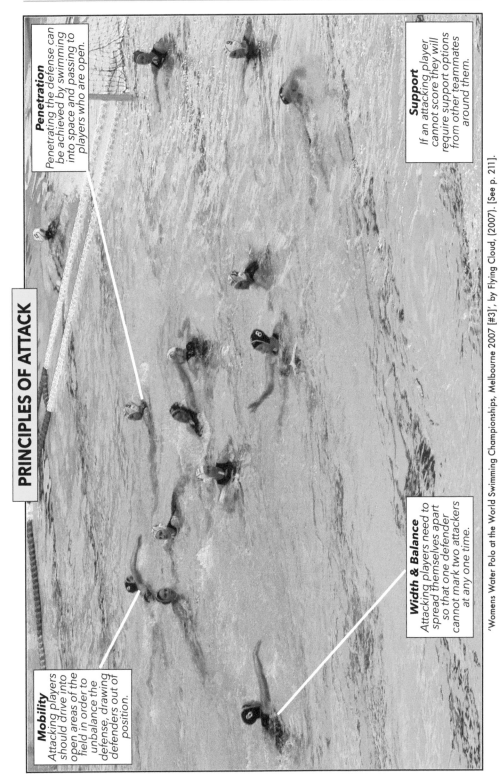

Penetration
Penetrating the defense can be achieved by swimming into space and passing to players who are open.

Support
If an attacking player cannot score they will require support options from other teammates around them.

Mobility
Attacking players should drive into open areas of the field in order to unbalance the defense, drawing defenders out of position.

Width & Balance
Attacking players need to spread themselves apart so that one defender cannot mark two attackers at any one time.

'Womens Water Polo at the World Swimming Championships, Melbourne 2007 [#3]', by Flying Cloud, (2007). [See p. 211].

backwards. Providing support is the key factor to moving the ball around in the attacking zone, which will deliver the dual benefit of disorienting the defense.

d. Mobility

Attacking players should drive into open areas of the field in order to unbalance the defense by drawing defenders out of position. Driving into open areas will have two possible outcomes. First, a defender follows the attacker and so space is created behind the defender, and second, the defender does not follow the attacker, in which case the attacker is now open to receive a pass or shoot.

e. Width & Balance

Attacking players need to spread themselves far enough apart so that one defender cannot cover or mark two attackers at once. This aspect of attacking is referred to as width and balance. Attacking players should also try to tempt defenders away from covering the more dangerous area in front of goal by using the full width of the field, stretching out the defensive shape.

f. Creativity

Attacking players should attempt to break down the defense by playing at an explosive pace to gain an element of surprise. An effective attacker should develop creativity and innovation in their attack and improvise where necessary (eg. baulking, fake passes etc.). Developing a repertoire of various types of shots that can be executed in different situations or from a wide range of locations across the field is a potent offensive capability.

46. Anticipation

Being able to anticipate the play is a critical skill that will assist all aspects of an attackers game. There are some

Anticipation

46

Skill Sequence:
1. Know how the ball reacts in & on the water;
2. Know the rules & always watch the ball;
3. Watch your teammates & the opponents
4. Always listen to and watch the referees

(Use of this image is licensed under Creative Commons).

phases of all water polo games where we can predict what the outcome of an action or phase of play might be. For example, you may know that a very competent teammate is adept at making interceptions, or you can see that your team will win that race for the ball. In these and many other phases of a game most players wait for an outcome to play out before moving to their next course of action, when anticipating the outcome ahead of time and moving beforehand can create greater opportunity.

A good example of anticipating the play is understanding what outcomes might possibly result from an attempted shot on goal. Any shot can result in four possible outcomes:

- *a goal (with a re-start at half-way);*
- *a corner throw (with a re-start at the corner on 2m);*
- *a rebound (and possible tussle for possession);*
- *a block by the goalkeeper (becoming a turnover).*

Being aware that there are only four possible outcomes from any attempted shot on goal, an outside defender breaking away on counter-attack at the moment a shot is being taken should know that they can achieve a considerable break without too much risk. Three of the four above possible outcomes are actually favourable to the defensive team going into counter-attack, and even if the outcome was a goal, there was no harm done in breaking away as you will be simply called back.

Players will also increase their ability to anticipate phases of the game the more they understand the rules, how the ball interacts with the water and many other relevant factors of reading a game. An ability to anticipate the play can also be heightened by carefully watching the ball, your teammates, the opponents, the shot clock and listening to the referees. Anticipating and thinking about what might happen next allows players to react quicker than their opponents.

47. Momentum

Momentum or how fast a match is played out is another important factor for an offensive team. The momentum of an attack depends upon how quickly each individual attacker acts and reacts. Swimming speed and reacting to play should always be conducted with intensity and high energy as this leaves less time for the defense to catch on to what is happening around them.

The momentum of an attack should also increase considerably as the ball approaches the attackers goal, culminating with the centre-forwards and drivers 'exploding' into a full assault. With less time to react the defense is much

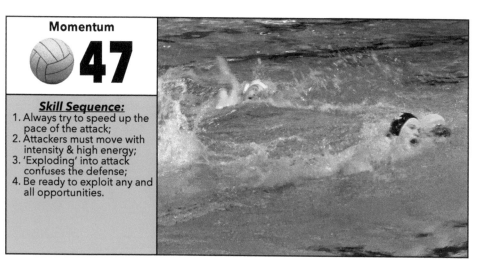

Momentum

47

Skill Sequence:
1. Always try to speed up the pace of the attack;
2. Attackers must move with intensity & high energy;
3. 'Exploding' into attack confuses the defense;
4. Be ready to exploit any and all opportunities.

less likely to slow the speed of an attack, and they are less able to concentrate and balance their defense. The end result is that the attacking team is much more able to exploit openings and opportunities by capitalising on errors in the defense.

48. Support

A common skill required in the offensive phases of any match is for attackers to support each other by making themselves open to receive passes. Easier to do with beginners, this skill becomes much harder to accomplish when pitted against more experienced defenders who actively try to shut down attackers by 'pressing' or tightly marking each player. However, there are a number of techniques that allow attacking players to provide supporting options for their teammates:

- *Be visible by swimming high in the water*
- *Communicate by calling to your teammates*
- *Sprint then perform 90^0 cut backs or square-outs*
- *Create pass options by moving into open space*
- *Present teammates with a clear line to pass*
- *Gain depth and width in supporting each other*
- *Drive on the ball side of defenders*

Attackers should constantly be in motion, always looking to swim into space to support and make themselves

Support

48

Skill Sequence:
1. Open yourself up by moving into space;
2. Sprint & perform 90^0 or 180^0 cut backs;
3. Drive into open space to provide teammates with passing options;
4. Achieve depth & width when attacking;
5. Help out any teammates who get caught.

'Passing under pressure & looking for support', by Malcolm Slaney, (28 Oct 2017). [See p. 211].

Driving Ability

49

Skill Sequence:
1. Pre-position yourself on the offensive perimeter;
2. Driving is about 'exploding' into action;
3. Use skills to get around your defender by surprise;
4. Always drive on the 'ball side' of your defender;
5. Be ready & open for a pass & shot if possible.

'Driver for Iran men's national water polo team [#2]', by Ansari, (2016). [See p. 211].

open to receive passes. An attacking player who remains stationary alongside their defender is actually making themselves an asset to the defense!

49. Driving

Once an attack has been established and the centre-forward is in the 'hole' position, an opportunity is present for attacking players to drive into the goal area. The explosive attack of a water polo driver is usually initiated and co-ordinated from a foul on the centre-forward. The objective of a drive can be: to gain an opportunity to shoot; to create a diversion; or move defenders out of position.

A driver can receive a pass from any teammate , but more often the pass will come from the centre-forward, who having been fouled is looking to find teammates that are open for taking a shot at goal.

Potential drivers should position themselves on the offensive perimeter and drive into the goal area at the right moment. A driver's first obstacle is to get around the defender using various techniques (*see Chapter 11: Offensive Tips & Tricks*). Once this is achieved the attacker drives toward goal before rearing up if open, to receive a pass and make an attempted shot. If that

Skill Sequence:
1. Build a range of attacking skills that can be used in different situations;
2. Develop a wide range of shots that can be used in different situations;
3. Be unpredictable when attacking.
4. Change tactics if you're not getting anywhere.

particular drive is unsuccessful and possession has been maintained, most attacks usually have time to reform and formulate a second or even third drive before the shot clock runs out.

50. Creativity

There are no specific skills that can be taught in relation to being creative in attack, but watching talented players is a great way of gaining inspiration. Often, the talent in executing a successful attack is to simply use a tactic that temporarily throws the defender off balance. Achieving surprise by incorporating a degree of imagination, resourcefulness and enterprise can be a powerful offensive weapon.

Being creative and innovative in attack includes using both legal and illegal methods of gaining an advantage, in the full knowledge that you could possibly be penalised for indiscretions. Whether its knowing when to perform a push-off, look in one direction and pass or shoot in another, or swim underwater to confuse the defense, being creative in attack is an important offensive capability. Effective and accurate shooting is an obvious and critical component of a creative attackers role and is the subject of the next chapter of this book (*see Chapter 9*).

51. Common Attacking Errors

Beginners and inexperienced players need to be aware of possible errors that members of an attack can unknowingly commit, which can disrupt an attack. Common mistakes that players can make when on offense include:

- *passing behind a breaking player, which causes that player to stop and go back, cancelling out the break;*
- *passing back to your goalkeeper, which allows the defense time to catch up and re-organise;*
- *dribbling the ball too far, which erodes good support and the shot clock, causing a deteriorating situation;*
- *throwing risky or optimistic passes, which introduces an element of uncertainty and turns possession into a free for all;*
- *throwing the ball into an area where the defense has a numerical advantage, which usually presents the defense with a turnover;*
- *attackers being too close together, which allows one defender to mark two or more attackers at the same time;*
- *having too many players on counter-attack, which can leave your defense exposed in the event of a turnover (eg. a three-on-one break is unnecessary);*
- *allowing a defender to reach over and push your hand and the ball underwater, which is a 'ball under foul' and presents the defense with a turnover;*
- *swimming into the 2m area when the ball is not inside the 2m, which is a '2m foul' and a turnover.*

Common Offensive Errors

51

Knowledge:
1. When engaged in any offensive phase, players need to be aware of the most common errors that members of an offense can unknowingly commit.

'The 5th test match at the AIS Aquatic Centre between Australia (white caps) women's national water polo team and Great Britain women's national water polo team. Australia won the test 14-3', by LauraHale, (28 Feb 2012). [See p. 211].

Pass Timing & Accuracy

The main factors to consider when passing to teammates are: that the pass is thrown when it is required; that the pass is accurate; and that the passer has the ability to deliver the ball over the required distance. Timing and accuracy are not difficult skills to acquire in themselves. The difficulty lies in being able to pass the ball accurately, while being put under pressure by the defense, and still deliver the pass at the right moment.

An effective pass should be well-timed to arrive at its intended destination, not before or after, but exactly when it is required by the receiver. In terms of accuracy, making an attempted shot easier for your teammate requires being able to deliver the ball exactly where it is required.

When working the ball up the field most passes should generally be made onto the water. In the attacking half and especially when working closer to the goal, passes need to be directed to a specific hand and at a height required by the receiver to assist with their impending shot. The importance of pass timing and accuracy cannot be overestimated.

Outnumber The Defense

A primary objective for any attacking team is to try and outnumber the defense or gain a numerical advantage at some point. The optimal situation for an offensive team is where an attacker shakes themselves free of any defenders and only has to shoot past the goalkeeper to score, known as a '1 on none' break. The next best situation is where two attackers share only one defender between them, known as a '2 on 1' break. The obvious objective being to pass the ball to the attacker who has the most favourable chance of scoring.

This numerical advantage can also work when the offensive team has three attackers against two defenders (3 on 2 break); and even four attackers against three defenders (4 on 3 break). But the advantage becomes increasingly less effective as the number of defenders escalates. Outnumbering the defense is not a difficult skill, but it does require an awareness to exploit promising attacking opportunities as they occur.

Attacking From Starts & Re-Starts

As starts, re-starts and set plays commence after a break in the play, they become phases of a water polo game where the offensive team can exploit the defense by executing pre-planned manouevres, otherwise known as 'set plays'. An effective offense should prepare for such opportunities by developing attacking strategies and routines right from the swim off. Offensive manouevres can be developed to exploit the defense following:

- *the swim off*
- *a restart after a goal has been scored against you*
- *a goal throw or free throw*
- *a corner throw*
- *a time-out*

▶*Offensive manouevres can be pre-planned to exploit the defense at set stoppages in play such as starts and restarts. 'Eger vs Vasas water polo game at Eger, Hungary, by sikeri, (12 Apr 2014). [See p.211].*

In all of the above situations offensive players should be aware of which manouevre or plan is being executed as well as when, and what their individual role in that strategy involves.

Summary

There are many other skills and techniques that can be practiced and performed for attacking in water polo, but the techniques outlined in this chapter are the more commonly used offensive skills for water polo players. After these skills have been introduced, practiced and mastered, they form the basic offensive skills for water polo athletes.

In the next chapter, players will learn how and when to best use shooting techniques and build a repertoire of shots to attack and score goals from different situations.

Checklist of Offensive Skills			
Skill #	Skill Name	✔	Date Mastered
45	Principles of Offense		
46	Anticipation		
47	Momentum		
48	Support		
49	Driving Ability		
50	Creativity		
51	Common Attacking Errors		

Chapter 9
SHOOTING SKILLS

'Water polo shooter', by Ankarino, (undated). [See p. 211].

"I never thought of the consequences of missing a big shot... when you think about the consequences you always think negative"
Michael Jordan

Why Shooting Skills Are Important

If you had to pinpoint one aspect of water polo that eclipsed all the others, it would have to be the ability to shoot and score goals. Amongst the many significant factors that make the most difference in any game, shooting has to be at the top of the list. Very simply, shooting skills are important because scoring goals wins games.

Good shooters can completely change the dynamics of an offense, making it easier to penetrate the defense and score more goals. Offensive minded coaches know that a few good shooters in the pool can work wonders for an attack, even if they don't score. Just by having the threat of a good shooter stretches out the defense and causes them to cover more ground.

Good shooters open up passing lanes for everyone on the team and make it easier to score. However, if nobody can shoot or a team has limited opportunity to score, then the opposite can occur and a defense will easily be able to compact their players to make scoring difficult. There are a number of factors that contribute to shooting effectiveness and the following section details a range of important considerations.

52. Working Into A Shooting Position

After regaining possession, but the counter-attack has failed, the team transitioning to offense will need to set up an organised attack. In order to develop and proceed with an assault, players should first work themselves into scoring positions and this can often be made difficult by a determined defense.

The offense needs to be spread apart and balanced in order to stretch the defense. Attacking players should understand that defenders are there to resist them and a degree of aggression may be necessary. Swimming as fast as possible and employing explosive all out attacking movements will assist the offense by reducing the time available for the defense to react.

Field position that will best advantage an attacker would be to keep their defender either behind them or at their side. This means gaining a position closer to the goal than the defender, or closer to their teammate with the ball than the defender.

Although illegal, small underwater touches and push-offs against defenders can often help to achieve better positioning for a shot. When the ball does arrive, attackers

Working Into Position

 52

Skill Sequence:
1. Attacking explosively will unbalance the defense;
2. Always attack aggressively and always at speed;
3. Keep your defender at your side if possible;
4. Drive into the goal area on the ball side of a defender;
5. Small push-offs & touches can assist your positioning;
6. Know what to do before you receive the ball.

'Partido de Waterpolo en Jaén, España [#2100]', by Juan Fernández, (2 Dec 2007). [See p. 211].

Shooting Effectiveness

53

Knowledge:
1. Body Position;
2. Strength;
3. Accuracy;
4. Speed & Power;
5. Surprise;
6. Distance;
7. Disguising & Faking;
8. Shot Selection;
9. The Goalkeeper;
10. The Cross Pass.

'Water Polo shooter [3X9A4928]', by Malcolm Slaney, (undated). [See p.211].

should be prepared to receive the pass and quickly execute their best shot. If a scoring opportunity doesn't occur, attackers should swim sideways out of the attacking zone and not clutter the area in front of goals, then circulate around for another attack.

53. Shooting Effectiveness

Being an effective shooter involves several important factors:

a. Strength

Attackers need to develop both mental and physical strength to overcome the close attention they will no doubt receive from vigorous defenders and their attempts to prize the ball loose.

b. Body Position

In preparing to take a shot at goal, a players body position is critical to the outcome. Shooters should achieve height out of the water, lean slightly forward, elbow clear of the water and execute the throw with an explosive shooting action.

c. Speed & Power

Power is a measure of how much energy is created, the amount of force used to shoot and the velocity at which it is delivered. Naturally the harder a ball is thrown, the more difficult it is to track. Combined with accuracy, a water polo ball should be thrown at the maximal controllable speed.

d. Surprise

Incorporating elements of surprise into a shot markedly increases the chances of success, especially when combined with speed and accuracy. Throwing an unexpected or unusual shot can often catch the defense completely off guard.

e. Distance

Scoring is generally more effective when the offense gets as close to the goal as possible. If an attacker finds themselves at 7m with no one open for a pass, they should dribble the ball in to 4m or less to decrease the throwing range and increase their probability of scoring.

f. Disguising & Faking

To make the goalkeeper's job even more difficult, shooters should develop methods of concealing their intentions eg. looking or leaning to one side and shooting to the other, or even looking completely away to be followed by an immediate quick shot (*see Faking & Baulking #55*).

▶Knowing that the top and bottom corners are the most difficult places for goalkeepers to reach, a shooter should still look at the goal and the goalkeeper's position within the goal. (Licensed under a Creative Commons.

◀For the 'push shot' keep the throwing elbow high throughout and increase power by pushing from the shoulder. If you have time, fake a shot to throw the goalkeeper off, before sending the ball to the other side of the goal.

g. Shot Selection

The type of shot thrown will depend on any number of factors including how much space and time there is. Developing a 'repertoire' of shots that can be executed in different situations from a wide range of locations, is a useful and potent offensive capability. Successful shooting requires selecting the right shot for the right situation eg. a power shot from 6m, a lob across the goal from the left side, an unexpected backhand or an off the water shot if being closely trailed by a defender.

h. The Goalkeeper

Players should quickly glance at the goal before shooting to guage the goalkeeper's position, then aim the shot accordingly, which should usually be at any of the four corners, or the most exposed part of the net.

j. Accuracy

Visualizing where a shot will be directed is an important factor in preparing to shoot. Before throwing, an attacker should look at the goal and the goalkeeper's position within the goal. Aim the shot at the most exposed part of the net, which is usually into any of the four corners (top or bottom) or sometimes above the goalkeeper's head, but ensuring that the shot is within the frame of the goal gives your attempted shot a chance.

j. The Cross Pass

Shooters should also be aware of the position of their teammates, with a cross pass to a better placed player often being a much more effective option than winding up for an individual shot. For example, with defenders and the goalkeeper firmly locked onto the shooter, giving an accurate cross pass to an undefended teammate can often achieve the same outcome easier.

As a final note, adhering to these suggestions should increase scoring effectiveness, which will in turn improve shooting percentages. It is important that even a small improvement in shooting percentage will bestow a tremendous advantage upon their team with more winning games as a result.

Shooters be aware of their other players, with a cross pass to a teammate often being a much more effective option than winding up for an individual shot.

Performing a Shot

54

Skill Sequence:
1. Use vigorous egg-beater kick;
2. Start by angling the body backwards at the hips;
3. Non-throwing shoulder slightly forward;
4. Transfer your weight from back to front as you throw;
5. Shooting arm high with elbow clear of the water;
6. Throw with the shoulder, elbow, wrist & fingers;
7. Ball leaves the hand with a backwards spin

54. Performing a Shot

Being able to establish a solid platform for a shot at goal will impact greatly on how the shot is performed as well as the final result. A powerful shot can only result from a combination of being balanced, high out of the water, and using great strength.

a. Shooting Technique

When about to make an attacking shot, players should be vigorously performing egg-beater kick to achieve height out of the water. As the ball is received a shooter should slightly angle their body with the non-throwing shoulder pointing toward the goal, while the shooting arm and elbow are kept well clear of the water.

A shot results from the body sequentially contracting beginning at the legs and hips, the abdomen and is then followed by the shoulders. The non-throwing shoulder jerks backwards while the throwing shoulder is whipped forward. The momentum should build from one body part to the next, be carried on at the elbow by the forearm, then at the wrist by the hand, and conclude with a forceful downward snap of the fingers to release a backward spinning ball.

ANANLYSIS OF SHOOTING TECHNIQUE

Visualise the Shot
Visualize where you are going to shoot. Before throwing look at the goal and the goalkeeper's position within the goal. Aim the shot at the most exposed part of the cage.

Egg-beater Kick
When about to shoot, players should be vigorously performing egg-beater kick to achieve height out of the water.

Elbow Out Of Water
A shooter should slightly angle their body with their non-throwing shoulder pointing at the goal, while the shooting arm and elbow are kept well clear of the water.

'Brendan Fisher, takes a practice shot to warm up for the UC Irvine vs Cal Lutheran match', by Chris Hunkeler, (undated). [See p. 211].

◀The achieve the correct sequence and timing for shooting a water polo ball, a shooter must attain maximal release velocity by beginning the shot in the toes and ending it in the fingertips. The force being generated by one part of the body is built upon by the force of the next part, until the final release, which ends with a snap of the fingertips. Neil LeVecke (LMU) plays in the Long Beach State vs Loyola Marymount match, score 11-7, by Chris Hunkeler, (undated). [See p. 211].

Two other technical, but important factors to consider when shooting are the principles of 'transfer of weight' and 'summation of forces'.

b. Transferring Weight

This factor refers to a situation where a player leans out of balance, or places their weight in one direction and then quickly shifts it to another direction, thereby 'transferring their weight'. An example of this is a baseball hitter loading up on their back foot to swing at a pitched ball and they transfer their weight forward to make the hit. Another example is a rugby player crouching low before springing forward and transferring weight into a tackle. Water polo players do the same thing when throwing or shooting the ball, as they transfer weight from behind to ahead of their shoulder line when shooting.

c. Summation of Forces

This factor becomes more relevant when several joints are used in the performance of a skill as their sequence and timing are important. The principle of 'summation of forces' begins with big muscle groups and moves progressively outwards through the smaller muscles. The continuous flowing movement is produced by forces created by different muscle groups that build upon each other to accumulate momentum, in order to perform the skill with greater force.

The force generated by one part of the body is built on by the force of the next part, which incorporates the next subsequent joints and so on. In throwing a water polo ball, the hip action commences just as the leg extension decelerates. The shoulder action commences as the hip rotation decelerates and so on. The release velocity of the ball will therefore depend on the speed of the last part of the body to launch the throw. The correct sequence and timing allows a shooter to attain maximal release velocity by beginning the shot in the toes and ending in the fingertips.

d. Accuracy

Winning in water polo means scoring goals, so the goal-frame naturally becomes the target when shooting. But the

A powerful shot can only result from a combination of being balanced, high out of the water, and using great strength. 'Hungary vs Holland water polo match at the XXII Olympiad, Moscow, 1980,' by Vladimir Vyatkin, (10 Jul 1980). [See p. 211].

WHERE TO SHOOT AT GOAL

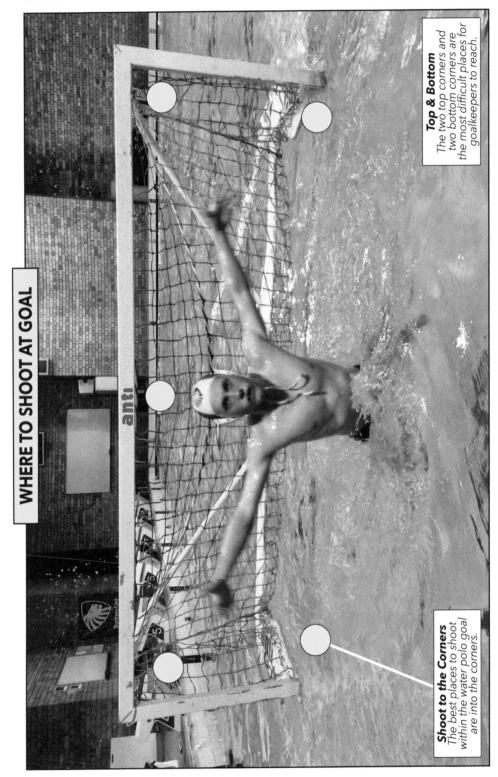

Top & Bottom
The two top corners and two bottom corners are the most difficult places for goalkeepers to reach.

Shoot to the Corners
The best places to shoot within the water polo goal are into the corners.

area of a water polo goal is around 2.8m², so within that large space, where is the best place to shoot? We need to remember that the goal is defended by a goalkeeper, whose presence is all about stopping anything from going into the cage.

Of course, the better the goalkeeper, the harder it will be to score goals, but generally the best places to shoot are into the corners of the goal. The two top corners and two bottom corners are the most difficult places for goalkeepers to reach so placing an accurate shot in any of those four zones should yield results more often. Shooting under the goalkeepers arms or above their head can also secure goals, but a shooter needs to be very accurate to score in these locations.

e. Shooting Percentage

Shooting percentage is defined as the number of goals scored, divided by the number of attempts to score, and is a useful statistic to record for individual players as well as teams. As an example, how many attempted shots would be required to score 12 goals?

If 'Team A' has a 40% shooting percentage (ie, they score 4 out of every 10 attempts), they'll have to generate about 30 attempts on goal to score 12 goals. But if 'Team B' is shooting at 60% then they'll only need to generate 20 shots on goal! Obviously, shooting at a higher percentage doesn't require as many scoring opportunities, meaning less shots on goal, which makes winning easier.

55. Faking & Baulking

Another necessary skill for attacking players is to possess an effective fake or baulk. A good fake shot is a skill that will help players extend their game from being good, to becoming great water polo performers. Possessing the ability to draw a defender or a goalkeeper by baulking or faking a shot before passing to a better placed teammate can bag many goals.

Faking & Baulking

55

Skill Sequence:
1. Set up for taking a normal shot;
2. Look and act dangerous, with every intent to shoot;
3. Pump the ball back & forth, or from side to side;
4. Try to draw the defense or goalie to you;
5. Pass off, or shoot if the defense doesn't respond.

A pump fake (also known as a baulk) is held in exactly the same way as a normal shot, but the ball is moved back and forward in a baulking or pumping fashion. A skilled performer also varies the speed of the fake, from slow to quick, or they stop then pump again etc. The key to a good fake shot is to act with an intent to shoot, making the fake look as convincing as possible. Performing a good baulk or fake shot requires virtually the same lead-up as you would perform for a real shot. If the defense doesn't respond and you are left open, then move-in closer and shoot if necessary.

56. Standard Shots

The most commonly used shots can be classified as 'standard' shots, which include: the swim in and pick up off the water shot; the lob shot; and the shot from a cross pass onto the hand. These types of shots can be performed from left or right sides of the field, but the target will change depending on the shooting angle. These shots are most effective when there are no trailing defenders and the attackers have both time and space to execute the shot without too much interference.

☑ **STANDARD PICK UP SHOT.** The most commonly used shot in the game, which is relatively easy to perform by lifting the upper body, shoulder, shooting arm and ball clear of the water. Ball should be thrown with maximal speed from any part of the field. *Tip - lean into the shot.*

☑ **LOB SHOT.** A relatively easy shot to perform into the far corner of the goal over the goalkeepers head. Should be thrown with accuracy usually from the sides of the pool (RH from left & LH from the right). *Tip - draw the goalie forward by pump faking a hard shot before lobbing.*

☑ **CROSS PASS & SHOT** (from the preferred side). This shot is caught from a cross-pass from the preferred side to catch the goalkeeper out of position. Relatively easy to perform and should be thrown with accuracy. Use cross-pass shots to beat good goalkeepers. *Tip - shoot as quick as possible into the open corner of the goal.*

☑ **CROSS PASS & SHOT** (from the non-preferred side). The ball is again caught from a cross-pass, but received across the body from the non-preferred side. Relatively easy to perform and should be thrown with accuracy. Use cross-pass shots to beat good goalkeepers. *Tip - shoot as quick as possible into the open corner of the goal.*

☑ **5M FREE THROW SHOT.** A relatively easy shot to perform after being fouled outside the 5m line and uses the standard pick up shot. Should be thrown with maximal speed. *Tip - the 5m throw must be performed in one motion immediately after being fouled.*

Standard Shots **56**	
Knowledge: The 'standard shots' are most effective when there are no trailing defenders and the attackers have both time and space to execute the shot without too much interference.	

'Determined to get the shot away', by Malcolm Slaney, (28 Oct 2017). [See p. 211].

Off The Water Shots

 57

Knowledge:
'Off the water' shots are most effectively used when there are trailing defenders ready to knock down a raised arm or the attackers don't have the time or space to execute a standard shot.

57. Off The Water Shots

Also relatively easy to perform, but not as common nowadays is a category known as 'off-the-water' shots, by virtue of the fact that they can be performed when the ball is on the surface of the water. These types of shots can be performed from left or right sides of the field, but the target will change depending on the shooting angle. They are most effectively used when there are trailing defenders ready to knock down a raised arm or the attackers don't have the time or space to execute a standard shot.

For off-the-water shots, the attacker can generally maximise power by drawing the ball closer in to the body and by keeping the elbow of the shooting arm high. They tensd to be more effective when disguised by combining a normal swimming action with the launching motion of the shot.

☑ **PUSH SHOT.** A handy shot to use after gaining inside water. Moderately easy to perform with practice. Should be pushed accurately when driving straight toward the goal. *Tip - keep the throwing elbow high throughout and increase power by pushing from the shoulder, and if you have time, fake a shot to throw the goalkeeper off, before sending the ball to the other side of the goal.*

☑ **BAT or T-SHOT.** Another handy shot to use after gaining inside water. Moderately easy to perform with practice. Should be batted with force and accuracy when driving straight toward the goal. _Tip - keep the batting elbow high throughout and increase power by using a breast-stroke kick, and batting from the shoulder. Blend the shot into your increased rate of stroke to surprise the goalkeeper._

☑ **BACKHAND SHOT.** A useful, but often inaccurate shot as the thrower has their back to the goal. Difficult to perform well under pressure. The thrower should have a good understanding of where they are sitting in relation to the goal, the goalkeeper and their defender. The ball should be whipped with power as quick as possible. Use when a goalkeeper keeps coming out to intercept passes. _Tip - keep the ball at arms length, invert your hand under the ball, keeping the throwing elbow high and whip the ball backwards._

☑ **ROUND ARM or SCOOP SHOT.** Performed from the centre-forward position. For RH - extend the hand to cradle the ball on the right side, then scoop or round-arm the ball while spinning to the left in a centrifugal motion and release into the goal. Reverse for LH. _Tip - use egg-beater kick to lift yourself out of the water (similar to a discus throw)._

☑ **WRIST & SPIKE SHOT.** An unusual off the water shot, which throws the ball into the air with one hand, then spikes the ball into goal with the other open hand, like volleyball. Should be unexpected and rapidly performed. _Tip - use explosive eggbeater kick to gain height out of the water._

Use a 'subtle' push off from a nearby defender to assist when throwing the rearback shot.

Creative & Trick Shots

58

Knowledge:
'Creative and trick shots' are most effective when they are unexpected, or are delivered from an unusual location, which can catch the defenders and the goalkeeper off guard.

►*To perform the backhand shot, keep the ball at arms length, invert your hand inside and under the ball, keeping the throwing elbow high and whip the ball backwards.*

58. Creative & Trick Shots

From a spectator point of view, the most thrilling shots to watch, but most difficult to perform are termed 'creative and trick' shots, which include but are not limited to: the wrist and volley shot; the rear-back shot; the backhand spinning lob shot; the laying on the side shot; the bounce, skip or wrap shot; the deflection or flick-on shot; and trick shots with the foot. This is by no means a complete list as new creative shots and their variations are constantly evolving, being developed and performed. These types of shots can also be performed from left or right sides of the goal, but the target will change depending on the shooting angle. Creative and trick shots are most effective when they are unexpected, or are delivered from an unusual location, which can catch the defenders and the goalkeeper off guard.

☑ **LOOK AWAY SHOT.** A nice trick shot if you are good at faking. Similar to the standard shot and can be thrown from anywhere. After catching the goalkeepers attention, relax and look to a team mate (as if to pass), then immediately shoot at goal. *Tip - the 'look-away' needs to convince everyone that you're going to pass.*

☑ **SKIP or BOUNCE SHOT.** A commonly used power shot, which is relatively easy to perform by lifting the upper body, shoulder, shooting arm and ball clear of the water. The ball should be thrown with maximal speed onto the water to make it skip off the surface and travel in an upwards trajectory into goal. *Tip - aim the ball to skip about 1m to 2m short of the goalkeeper.*

☑ **REAR BACK SHOT.** Can be performed solo or from a cross-pass. The driver suddenly stops and rears back with the upper body, shoulder, shooting arm and ball clear of the water. Should be thrown with maximal speed from the attacking third of the field. *Tip - use egg-beater kick to rear up out of the water & use a 'subtle' push off from a close defender to assist.*

☑ **PULL ON SHOT.** This trick shot is caught from a cross-pass from the non-preferred side. A nice pre-planned shot to use after a time-out or stop in play. Drivers swim across the face of the goal and roll onto their back to receive high pass from teammates on the offensive perimeter. The shooter jumps high out of the water and both catches and pulls the ball into the goal all in the same movement. *Tip - the pass should be thrown with a good deal of force.*

☑ **WRIST FLICK SHOT.** A specialty trick shot that mimics a fake pump and fractionally delays the shot, which can put the goalkeeper off. Not generally used in matches, but can be thrown from anywhere inside the 5m zone. *Tip - requires excellent ball handling skills.*

The bounce or skip shot should be thrown with maximal speed onto the water to make the ball skip off the surface and travel in an upwards trajectory into goal. The trajectory of a skip or bounce shot. '[Wasserball Bären von Winterthur]', by Rio Werner Hauser, (28 Jan 2012). [See p.211).

◄Regardless of whether you are a beginner or an Olympic champion, slotting an accurately placed goal is one of the greatest pleasure's of participating in the sport of water polo. 'Water Polo played at Monmouth College water pool inside the Huff Center, UK', by Monmouth College, (5 Aug 2014). [See p.211].

☑ **HORIZONTAL SHOT.** An effective shot to get around the outstretched arms of defenders. The body should be almost horizontal in the water, allowing the throwing arm to pivot almost 2m from the hips and over the head. Accuracy is somewhat enhanced and the ball should be thrown with power. *Tip - balance by sculling with the non-throwing arm.*

☑ **BACKHAND SPINNING LOB SHOT.** A useful, but often inaccurate shot as the thrower has their back to the goal. Should be lobbed from the sides of the pool (RH from right & LH from the left). *Tip - spin the ball to deflect in if the goalkeeper happens to make contact.*

☑ **DEFLECTED SHOT.** A nice pre-planned shot to use after a time-out or stop in play. An outside driver throws a much harder pass than normal in the air, and at the centre-forward, who simply deflects the ball's direction. All the power comes from the passer/shooter from the outside perimeter while the amount of deflection is dependent on the hole person. *Tip - the deflection should be minimal and not take speed off the ball.*

☑ **FOOT SHOTS.** These are specialty trick shots that by their very nature will surprise any goalkeeper. Not generally used in matches, but can be kicked in from anywhere, if the opportunity arises. *Tip - lay in a horizontal position with hips on the surface. Requires excellent ball handling skills.*

☑ **UNDERARM SKIM or WRAP SHOT.** A skimming power shot, which is difficult to perform. The ball should be thrown with the hand underneath the ball with maximal speed, to skim along the surface like a stone. _Tip - meant to be thrown underneath a goalkeepers rising arm, requires excellent ball handling skills and power._

☑ **SPIN OUT SHOT.** This trick shot is caught from a cross-pass coming from the non-preferred side. The ball should be thrown with maximal speed, but is difficult to perform under pressure. After catching, the shooter initially spins away from the goal, but spins like a centrifuge in a circle to release the ball with power at the goal. Not generally used in matches. _Tip - elevate the torso out of the water to assist with a rapid spin._

Summary

There are many other skills and techniques that can be practiced and performed in relation to shooting in water polo, but the shots and skills outlined in this chapter are the most commonly used shooting skills for water polo players. After these skills have been introduced, practiced and mastered, they form the basic shooting skills for water polo athletes.

In the next chapter, players will be introduced to the specialised position of goalkeeper, and will learn how and when to make best use of goalkeeping skills as the mainstay of the defense.

► A tip for shooting success - don't just throw balls at the goal when performing shooting practice, but rather try to score on every single attempt, because... "you will do in a game as you do in practice". 'Kostas Genidounias gets ready to pass the ball off during the second quarter. The Trojans led the score at half time 8-3. Genidounias scored a total of five goals during the game', by Neon Tommy, (1 Dec 2012). [See p.211].

Checklist of Shooting Skills

Skill #	Skill Name	✔	Date Mastered
52	Working Into Position		
53	Shooting Effectiveness		
54	Performing a Shot		
55	Faking & Baulking		
56	Standard Shots:		
a	*Straight Shot*		
b	*Lob Shot*		
c	*Cross Pass & Shot (preferred side)*		
d	*Cross Pass & Shot (non-preferred side)*		
e	*5m Free Throw Shot*		
57	Off The Water Shots:		
a	*Push Shot*		
b	*Bat or T-Shot*		
c	*Backhand Shot*		
d	*Roundarm or Scoop Shot*		
e	*Wrist & Volley Shot*		
58	Creative & Trick Shots:		
a	*Look-away Shot*		
b	*Bounce or Skip Shot*		
c	*Rearback & Shot*		
d	*Pull On Shot*		
e	*Wrist Flick Shot*		
f	*Backhand Spinning Lob Shot*		
g	*Underarm Skim or Wrap Shot*		
h	*Foot Shot*		
i	*Deflected Shot*		
j	*Spin Out Shot*		
k	*5m Penalty Shot*		

Chapter 10
GOALKEEPING SKILLS

'Partido de Waterpolo en Jaén, España [#2131]', by Juan Fernández, (2 Dec 2007). [See p. 211].

"Never, never, never give up!"
Winston Churchill!

Why Goalkeeping Skills Are Important

Due to the alternating attacking and defensive phases of water polo most players find it hard to maintain a set position in the field. The one exception is the goalkeeper who occupies a designated position. As in football, while shooters are revered for their ability to score, goalkeepers are equally applauded and relied upon for their ability to stop the other team from scoring, usually as the last line of defense.

Goalkeepers need to develop two distinct components of their game, the mental and the physical. They need to be very determined, courageous, be able to take risks and place their body on the line against the opposition when required. They need to be able to 'read' the play better than anyone else to understand where possible threats will most likely develop. They also need to communicate with their teammates and guide them to where they can be most effective. Then be able to react and explode into action with speed and mobility when required. Finally, the goalkeeper has a major function in attack, particularly after re-gaining possession to help launch the counter-attack.

The Goalkeeper's Role

Although it has already been mentioned that developing a high degree of egg-beater proficiency is a major priority, of course the main role of a goalkeeper is to stop goals being scored. However, goalkeepers should try if able, to catch the ball rather than bat it away, as a caught ball effectively regains possession for their team. This is important because a shot that is batted away can unintentionally hand possession straight back to the attacking team.

As goalkeepers occupy a central viewing position at the rear of the field the secondary roles of a goalkeeper are: to communicate with and help organise the defense; to clean up any loose ball that may come into their immediate area; to hold the ball high to signify they have regained possession; and to try and send away a long, safe pass to initiate any counter-attack. As a summary, the roles of a goalkeeper are:

Goalkeeping requires a special mental courage and determination that makes goalies place the welfare of their team above their own personal safety. 'Goalie James Clark blocks an attempt at the goal. Clark blocked a total of four goals during the first half of the game', by Neon Tommy, (1 Dec 2012). [See p.211].

- *Must have very strong egg-beater kick*
- *Communicate with & organise the defense*
- *Raise themselves up to be a physical barrier*
- *Be the last line of defense for stopping shots*
- *Catch balls rather than block or bat them away*
- *Clean up all loose ball in the goal area*
- *Hold onto the ball after possession is gained*
- *Give long, safe passes to initiate the counter-attack*

The Mental Game

Water polo goalkeeping is a very tough position as their role involves pitting themselves and their body against opposition players who throw very fast and hard shots. Taking these hits requires a special mental courage and determination that by nature of the position leads them to place the welfare of their team above their own personal safety.

While most attacking players are taught to shoot at the corners of the goal and away from goalkeepers, wayward shots do inevitably come into contact with a goalkeeper's body, shoulders, head and face, and it is not uncommon to cringe when a goalkeeper receives a shot directly in the face.

Encountering these confronting situations is a real mental challenge, particularly when balls are thrown at high velocity. Laying their bodies 'on the line' sets the

◀*As goalkeepers occupy a central viewing position at the back of the field one of their principle roles is to communicate with and help organise the defense.*

59

Knowledge:
1. The goalkeeper needs to become a student of the game, develop skills for 'reading the play', and be able to anticipate what could happen next. 'Reading the game' will permit goalkeepers to guide the defensive unit into position to maintain a balanced resistance.

'Water Polo at Lake Macquarie [ICG 2014]. Photo taken at the 2014 Lake Macquarie International Children's Games in December 2014', by moetaz attalla, (10 Dec 2014). [See p.211].

goalkeeper apart from the rest of the team. Anticipating the play and watching the unfolding match developments, while always keeping one eye on the ball is another example of the significant mental alertness required of a goalkeeper. In this respect, water polo goalkeepers are a very special breed.

The Physical Game

Physically, a goalkeepers foundation skill is to be able to perform egg-beater kick better than anyone else. They need to generate fast foot speed to lift their bodies high out of the water and develop the endurance to remain out of the water for longer periods. They also need to develop a proficiency at jumping up and out of the water to block shots by creating a physical barrier of arms, body and head. Possessing quick reaction skills and an ability to throw long safe passes are other highly valued individual skills for the goalkeeper.

59. Reading The Game

A goalkeeper should never take their eyes off the ball as a shot can come from anywhere in the field at anytime. The goalkeeper needs to become a student of the game, develop skills for 'reading the play', and be able to anticipate what could happen next. Reading the play will permit goalkeepers to guide their defensive players into position to maintain a

A GOALKEEPER'S PREPARATION

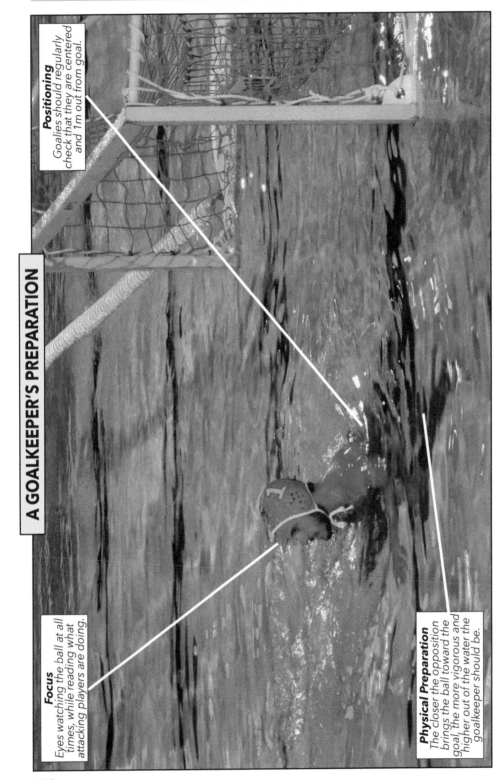

Positioning
Goalies should regularly check that they are centered and 1m out from goal.

Focus
Eyes watching the ball at all times, while reading what attacking players are doing.

Physical Preparation
The closer the opposition brings the ball toward the goal, the more vigorous and higher out of the water the goalkeeper should be.

balanced resistance.

Goalkeepers also need to: anticipate what attackers 'off the ball' might be trying to do; beware of possible 'outside' shots; guard against 'off the water' or lob shots; beware of players baulking or pump faking and whether a cross-pass might be possible; be aware of the capabilities of top shooters and where they position themselves; and anticipate an impending shot by thinking like a shooter. It's a lot of information to process in a constantly evolving setting, but a switched on goalkeeper is one of the greatest assets of a team.

60. Positioning

A goalkeeper being out of position is the cause of many goals, therefore a major factor that greatly contributes to a goalkeepers effectiveness is their ability to place and maintain themselves correctly in position, in relation to the goal.

An effective goalkeeper needs to be totally familiar with the dimensions of the goal and their position in

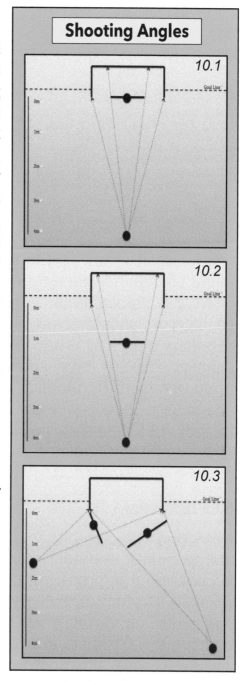

In guarding the goal, the keeper should never sit on the goal line (Fig. 10.1), but should move 1m forward to cut down the amount of exposed goal & the 'shooters angle' (Fig. 10.2). They should also square themselves accordingly to any threat coming from the sides of the field (Fig. 10.3).

179

Positioning

60

__Skill Sequence:__
1. Know & maintain your position in goals;
2. Reduce the goal area by moving towards shooters;
3. Keep checking your position in relation to goal;
4. Lead with the head around the goal arc;
5. Scull leaning forward, hands & hips on the surface.

relation to it. They should be aware of how their position might change depending on where the ball is coming from or what is known as the angle of attack. As a general rule, goalkeepers should always be out in front of the goal, and definitely not on or inside the goal line. They should square themselves to any threat and narrow down the shooting range of an opponent by moving about 1m forward of the goals (*compare Figure 10.1 with 10.2*). If shots are coming from the sides of the field the goalkeeper should adjust themselves to the angle and square themselves accordingly to the new threat (*see Figure 10.3*).

61. Preparation

In preparing to block shots a goalkeepers composure and technique shouldn't vary too much. A general rule to keep in mind in preparing for defense is that the closer the opposition brings the ball toward the goal, the more vigorous and higher out of the water the goalkeeper should become, which may culminate in a jump to catch and save the shot. The best body position for performing this preparation while maintaining an eye on both the game and the ball, is to lean forward and scull vigorously with hands close to the surface. As the ball is brought closer, the goalkeepers foot speed increases with the hips rising close up to the surface.

GOALKEEPING BASICS

Square to the Shooter
The goalkeeper should adjust themselves to the angle and square themselves to the threat accordingly.

Physical Barrier
Prevent shots and stop goals being scored by presenting a physical barrier of arms, body and head.

Strong Egg-beater Kick
Vigorous egg-beater foot speed increases and culminates in a jump or lunge to block or catch any ball.

'Womens Water Polo at the World Swimming Championships, Melbourne 2007 [#2]', by Flying Cloud, (2007). [See p. 211].

Preparation

61

London 2012

Skill Sequence:
1. Use a very powerful egg-beater kick;
2. Increase foot speed with hips on the surface;
3. Increase height out of the water as the ball nears;
4. Straighten at the hips, jump & extend the arms, vigorous egg-beater kick;
5. Always be ready to swim out and intercept

'GBR Water polo goalkeeper' by openDemocracy, (2012). [See p. 211].

The vigorous sculling and egg-beater foot speed gradually increases and usually culminates in a jump or lunge to catch or block any thrown ball, before it enters the goal.

62. Making The Save

Having been somewhat relaxed during the attack phase the goalkeeper should mentally prepare for the task ahead on the change of possession. Generally speaking, the closer the ball comes to the goal, the less contribution the goalkeepers arms will make and the greater the contribution becomes from their legs when defending any potential shots. They

Making the Save

62

Skill Sequence:
1. Mentally focus on the task ahead;
2. Keep hands on the surface and at the ready;
3. Always focus on the ball, not the shooter;
4. Jump as the shot is released, not before;
5. Try to catch the ball with both hands, not bat away;
6. Extend & absorb the ball force & pull ball down;
7. Then protect the ball & look to pass upfield to the counter-attack.

'About to score', by Three Peanuts, (undated). [See p. 211].

should be aware of what the attack is doing and monitor their own position in the goal, but must also continually watch the ball. As the ball is moved around the field the goalkeeper should lead with the head around the arc of the goal.

With one eye on the developing situation, the goalkeeper should be watching the ball and if and when a shot is imminent, they should move toward the shooter and jump when the ball is released. What happens after that is critical to gaining and maintaining possession.

Their task is to collect the ball if possible by either catching it or absorbing the power of the shot and allowing it to drop onto the water to then be quickly smothered and protected. A goalkeeper should try to avoid batting a ball away or deflecting it back into play as the opposition may then regain possession and continue the attack. Care should also be taken not to push the ball underwater as this may result in a penalty to the attacking team.

For close-in shots to the head or body, goalkeepers should try to absorb and block using two hands if possible, allowing the ball to drop down onto the water in front of them. Any one arm blocks at the extremities should also absorb the power of the shot and allow the ball to drop onto the water.

▶The goalkeeper should either try to catch or absorb the power of the shot, allowing the ball to drop onto the water, but any save that stops a goal is gold! 'Lake Macquarie International Children's Water Polo Games', by moetaz attalla, (10 Dec 2014). [See p.211].

Goalkeeper in Attack

63

Skill Sequence:
1. Aid the attack by quickly recovering the ball;
2. Control the speed of the counter-attack;
3. Goalie should hold the ball high & look to pass;
4. Goalies must always make a safe pass down field;
5. Pass priority is first long, then to the side;
6. Dribble the ball out if teammates are marked;
7. Re-set your defensive position after passing.

Defending lob shots taken from the sides of the pool requires the goalkeeper to take a backstroke arm pull to move backwards and pluck the ball out of the air with the opposite hand. After a save, the goalkeeper should make sure their area is secure, before resuming the basic alert or ready position.

63. The Goalkeeper In Attack

Once possession has been regained the goalkeeper becomes the key player in launching the counter-attack. Even though a counter-attack may have already commenced, the goalkeeper can control the speed and direction of the offensive by passing or withholding the ball. They should hold the ball high to indicate they have regained possession and look for the best passing option.

Their first priority should be to send a long pass down field or pass to the sides of the pool as a second choice if the long pass option is not possible. It is critical that passes from the goalkeeper are safe and can't be contested. To achieve this they should maintain eye contact with and call to whoever they are passing to, alerting them to the arrival of the ball. If teammates are marked, the goalkeeper can dribble the ball down field to try and break up the defense, or even take a shot, but rules state that goalkeepers must not progress over the half-way line. Once the ball is successfully moving down field, the goalkeeper should re-position themselves in the goals and prepare for the next defensive phase.

Goalkeeping Practice

As with most physical skills, ability generally improves with practice, and will improve quicker with more practice, especially 'perfect' practice. After learning the correct techniques, a goalkeepers ability to save goals will rapidly improve if provided with sufficient practice. Indeed, their rate of improvement is often a function of how many attempted shots they face in practice and in games (*see Figure 10.4*). One of the most important factors in developing good goalkeepers is to face as many shots as possible, which will in turn develop an understanding of how players shoot, how to move and how best to react in the goals.

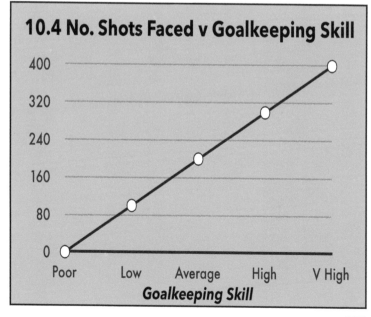

▶*Fig. 10.4 A goalkeepers' ability to save goals will usually improve if provided with sufficient practice. Their rate of improvement is often a function of how many attempted shots they face in practice as well as games.*

Summary

There are many other skills and techniques that can be programmed and performed for preparing goalkeepers in water polo, but the techniques outlined in this chapter are the most commonly used skills and techniques for water polo goalkeepers. After these skills have been introduced, practiced and mastered, they form the basic elements for water polo goalkeepers.

In the final chapter, players will learn how and when to best use shortcuts, trick techniques and tried and tested tips to save energy and improve their overall water polo playing effectiveness.

Checklist of Goalkeeping Skills			
Skill #	Skill Name	✔	Date Mastered
59	Reading the Game		
60	Positioning		
61	Preparation		
62	Making the Save		
63	The Goalkeeper in Attack		

Chapter 11
WATER POLO SECRETS & TIPS

'Romania psyching up prior to the USA v Romania match at the London Olympic Games',
by Alex Lomas, (31 July 2012). [See p. 211].

WATER POLO TIPS & TRICKS...

"Impossible is a word to be found only in the dictionary of fools"
Napoleon Bonaparte

Why Tips & Tricks Are Important

The skills presented in this final chapter are more applicable for players that have progressed through the beginning stages of water polo and are looking to enhance their existing ability and skills. Once players enter an intermediate stage of skill development they have often 'automated' many basic skills. At this point they are more open to learning refinements that allow them to adopt and perform skills quicker and generally achieve a higher degree of physiological efficiency.

This final chapter introduces a number of suggested techniques and tips that have been developed and performed by international water polo athletes over many years, which may assist novice players to gain an advantage. Right from the outset, it should be stated that some of these suggestions are illegal and not sanctioned by the rules of the game. However, if these techniques are applied at the right time and place, the benefit derived can outweigh the risk of detection and gain significant advantage for players over their opponents.

64. Competing In The Water

As water polo is the only invasion team game contested in the water, different methods have evolved for moving about, contesting for the ball and making body contact in order to compete effectively in what is essentially a weightless environment.

For example, it takes much longer to swim around a water polo field than to run around a basketball court, however, the speed of passing and shooting is exactly the same! This means that different defensive, swimming and offensive techniques have had to change, adapt and evolve over time in order to compete in a fluid environment.

Understanding how buoyancy and streamlining in the water assists movement, and how water resistance limits movement, is an important feature of water polo. This concept slows down some aspects of the game, while having no affect whatsoever on others. Other factors that may differentiate between athletes when they are equally matched in skill can include: anticipation; age; experience; reaction time; speed, strength and power; fitness; stage of skill development; and deception skills etc.

Competing in Water

64

Knowledge:
1. Exploring & understanding how buoyancy and streamlining assists movement, and how water resistance limits movement, is an important feature of water polo. Other factors that may differentiate between athletes when they are equally matched in skill include: anticipation; age; experience; reaction time; speed, strength and power; fitness; stage of skill development; and deception skills etc.

Defensive Phase

65

Tips & Tricks:
a. Passing Lanes;
b. Ball Under;
c. No Fouls;
d. Pressure;
e. Overpower;
f. Hinder;
g. Never Assist;
h. Swimsuit Hold;
i. Push Out.

The 30 'tips and tricks' included in this final chapter have been organised into defensive, swimming, offensive and goalkeeping phases. Each featured tip has a detailed description, and the 'tips and tricks' are further classified as being either legal (green) or illegal (red) under FINA rules.

65. Defensive Phase

There are a number of tricks in the defensive phase that players can use to create an advantage:

PASSING LANES. *While remaining close to the opponent you're guarding, defenders should be aware to try and occupy any potential passing lanes to mainly deter passes or make interceptions if possible.*

BALL UNDER. *A defensive ploy to regain possession is to be close enough to an opponent to reach over their arm or shoulder, at the exact moment they place their hand on the ball, then force their hand and the ball together underwater. As the attacker is technically in control of the ball, the rules state that they have taken the ball underwater while being challenged, which results in a turnover and free throw to the defense.*

NO FOULS. *Pressuring an opponent without fouling will make attempts to pass much more difficult, and this tactic also runs* the 'shot clock' down much quicker, giving the offense less time to score. To do this effectively, remain in body contact with your opponent so that they know you are there, but show both hands to the referee to indicate that you can't possibly be fouling.

PRESSURE. *Pressuring an opponent means to leave them with no space to manouevre by swimming on their back, swimming very close or to be in direct body contact, which will make their attacking efforts and progress upfield much more difficult.*

OVERPOWER. *It is important for a defender to always be higher in the water than their opponent, which is achieved by leaning forward and increasing the foot speed of their egg-beater kick.*

NEVER ASSIST. *Never assist the opposition by retrieving a ball when they receive a free throw. Even if it's right next to you just leave the ball alone as your otherwise very kind gesture could be penalised by the referees for possible interference.*

HINDER. *Defenders should make their opponents attempts to gain good field position difficult by blocking, pushing back, impeding and generally wearing offensive players down.*

Once players enter an 'intermediate stage of skill development' they have often 'automated' many basic skills and are more open to learning refinements of the game.

SWIMSUIT HOLD. *To keep an opponent close by and limit them from swimming around, grab hold of their swim suit with one hand, which will allow a defender to both watch the ball and know where their opponent is at the same time. This trick is often hard for the referee to detect.*

PUSH OUT. *Shots from attacking centre-forwards will be much more effective at 2m, so defenders should actively try to muscle their opponents (without using their hands) out of good scoring positions beyond 4m and 5m by using vigorous egg-beater kick.*

66. Swimming Phase

There are a number of tricks in swimming phases of the game that players can use to create an advantage:

KEEP MOVING. *Defenders really appreciate attacking players that stop swimming and just take up space, making them much easier to mark. To counteract this when attacking, keep swimming into the hole, across the goal, out to the wings etc., which will tire, confuse and unbalance the defense.*

BALL SIDE. *To minimise interceptions try to attack or drive on the ball side of your defender ie. put yourself between your teammate in possession of the ball and the defender that is guarding you.*

STOP & START. *A good trick which can result in either a small break, an ejection or a penalty against the defender. When driving into the hole get in front of your defender, then stop*

Swimming Phase

66

Tips & Tricks:
a. Keep Moving;
b. Ball Side;
c. Stop & Start;
d. Push Assist;
e. Underarm Slide;
f. Acting Foul;
g. Hip Swim;
h. Arm Check & Go.

'Zach Gleason (LMU) and Lee Griffin (LB) play in the Long Beach State vs Loyola Marymount match, score 11-7', by Chris Hunkeler, (undated). [See p. 211].

DRIVING ON THE BALL SIDE

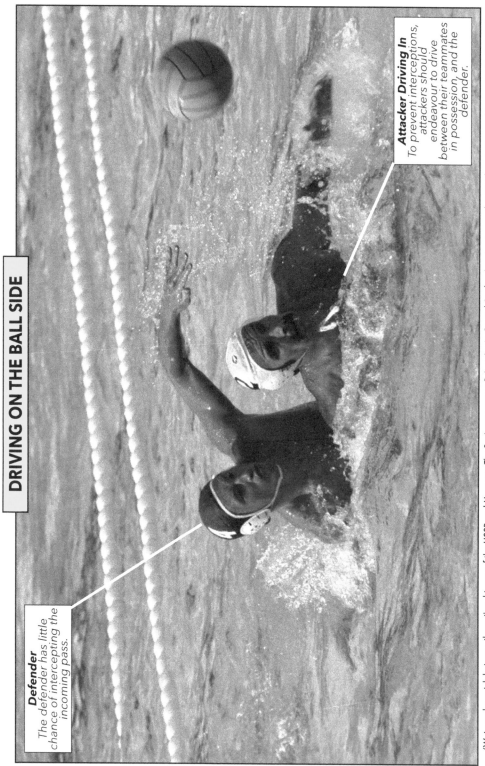

Attacker Driving In
To prevent interceptions, attackers should endeavour to drive between their teammates in possession, and the defender.

Defender
The defender has little chance of intercepting the incoming pass.

'Water polo match between the national teams of the USSR and Hungary. The Soviet team won 5-4, at Lenin Central Stadium's swimming pool, XXII Olympic Games. (Eugeny Grishin (#4-RUS) and Istvan Szivos (#2-HUN) fighting for a ball)', by Alexander Makarov, (1 July 1980). [See p. 211].

A standard principle for any team transitioning into attack is to try and gain a numerical advantage. Breaking players should aim for a one-on-none, a two-on-one or as shown above, a three-on-two advantage.

and let them run into you, then immediately take off again. If the defender is not ejected, you would have achieved inside water and gained a significant break.

PUSH ASSIST. *The push assist can be performed either at the swim off or anywhere in the field at anytime. This trick is accomplished by one player pushing their teammate along in the water either by cupping their hand as a stirrup to push off from, or by grabbing and forcing their teammates leg or thigh to help propel them through the water.*

UNDERARM SLIDE. *A great way to have your opponent ejected for 20 seconds and gain the advantage of an extra-man is to perform the underarm slide. Swimming at the same speed as, and alongside your opponent, just slip under the arm closest to you as they make their freestyle arm recovery, and then immediately slow up so that they end up on top of you.*

ACTING FOUL. *Drawing a free throw or better still an ejection against your opponent can often be achieved by simply acting like you have been fouled. The degree of success depends on how convincing you can be and how well you time its context.*

HIP SWIM. *Particularly effective if you're being beaten by a fast swimmer. Simply use your forearm to press down on their hips every time you take a stroke. This gives you a slight lift and slows them down by disrupting their swimming rhythm.*

ARM CHECK & GO. *A nice trick to gain a small break when driving. When swimming alongside a defender, speed up so that your shoulder and their head are in alignment then stop your arm vertically in mid-recovery. When their recovering arm makes contact with yours, quickly force their arm back and then take off at full speed. They are usually so surprised that they stop while you churn off ahead of them.*

67. Offensive Phase

There are a number of tricks in the offensive phase of the game that players can use to create an advantage:

GIVE & GO. *This technique is known as a 'give & go' because you start driving immediately after handing off a pass. This trick is intended to catch your defender off guard and give you a nice break right in the goal area.*

SELFIE FREE THROW. *Players can be penalised for wasting time in water polo, which often occurs when a player with a free throw has no one open to send their pass. To avoid incurring a foul for taking too long to take the free throw (3 seconds), just throw the ball up about 30cm to yourself and catch it to restart play and avoid a time wasting foul. Note that after taking your own free throw, you can't shoot at goal.*

LEG FEND. *Fending off from defenders with the feet is easy to do, but produces a big push-off, which is often detected by the referees. But just using the knee or the shin can still be an effective fend-off without exposing yourself too much to a foul.*

Offensive Phase

67

Tips & Tricks:
a. Give & Go;
b. Selfie Free Throw;
c. Leg Fend;
d. 90° Turn Out;
e. Twister;
f. Pull Through;
g. Centre-Back Flick.

'Water Polo Hole', by Ryanjo, (4 Jul 2006). [See p. 211].

EXTRA-MAN STRATEGY

Balanced & Concentrated Defence (Blue Caps)
The defense is reduced to 5 field players after an ejection, but a disciplined strategy will prevent the offensive team from scoring.

Move The Ball
A winning strategy for the attack is for all team members to be in a scoring position, and to quickly pass the ball around.

Extra Attacker (White Caps)
With one extra player, the offensive team has a temporary numerical superiority, known as 6 on 5.

'Womens water polo game at the Athens Olympic Games, 2004', by Maksim, [Prisonblues], (2004). [See p. 211].

90⁰ TURN OUT. *Swim and muscle your defender towards the corner of the pool before performing a 90⁰ turn-out to swim away in another direction. A cleaner break can be achieved by placing your hand against the defenders hip as you peel away, which stops their momentum and propels you to the side even quicker.*

TWISTER. *A technique to gain inside water against an aggressive defender or centre-back. From a face to face start, turn 180⁰ and roll your back up against the defenders chest, then hook your trailing elbow or forearm up under their armpit and quickly reverse direction to turn them around behind you, which should result in you having gained inside water.*

PULL THROUGH. *A technique to get past a particularly obstinate defender who is squared up in front of you and blocking your progress. Match your left arm with their right arm and quickly grab their extended wrist. Pull their wrist under your right armpit and at the same time take a long stroke with your right arm. This trick should be made to look like you're just taking a stroke, while the defender is left floundering as you swim past to gain inside water.*

CENTRE-BACK FLICK. *The centre-forward can use this trick to have their defender ejected, but they should first make sure the referees have their eyes on the ball and not on you. With the center-back behind and their hands raised (showing the referees they're not fouling), reach across and over your shoulder, grab their wrist, then sink and pull the defender over the top of you, while struggling to simulate a foul.*

68. Goalkeepers

There are a number of tricks that goalkeepers can use to create an advantage:

OFFSET SAVE. *Make one side of the goals appear to be bigger than the other side by positioning yourself slightly offset. Then be prepared to jump to the slightly larger side. This simple tip will often encourage players into shooting into the centre of the larger gap, from where the savvy goalkeeper is much better prepared to make the jumping save.*

PICK A SIDE. *Knowing full well that it is difficult to defend the entire goal, goalkeepers should practice choosing and blocking just one side only, which will give them at least a 50/50 chance of success.*

197

Goalkeepers

68

Tips & Tricks:
a. Offset Save;
b. Pick a Side;
c. Watch the Eyes;
d. Jamming Down;
e. Saving a Lob;
f. Ball Steal.

'Golakeeper preparing for an 'offset save'. Frame extracted from miniDV movie taken May 2005 at a high school water polo match', by Ryanjo, (8 Apr 2006). [See p. 211].

WATCH THE EYES. *At the beginning to intermediate level, most attacking players will look towards the spot they're preparing to shoot, which can give a savvy goalkeeper a nice warning signal as to where the ball will most probably be thrown.*

JAMMING DOWN. *Water polo players very soon find out that the best places to shoot are often the bottom corners of the goal as the goalkeeper rises up out of the water. Jamming down is a technique goalkeepers use to unexpectedly jump forward and down to stop shots in the lower corners.*

LOB SAVE. *The lob save is designed to cover as much of the goal as possible. Once you realise the attacking player has thrown a lob shot, begin doing backstroke across the goal and make the save with the outside hand, keeping your eyes on the ball at all times.*

BALL STEAL. *A talented goalkeeper will always be aware and ready to 'explode' out of their goal to make an interception or clean up a stray ball. Knowing your ability and gaining experience in all circumstances will improve your ability to steal the ball.*

Extra Man Strategy

The multiple variations of 'extra man' (6 on 5) attack and defense that can be pre-planned and performed after a defending player is ejected, form a major part of water polo. However, the tactics and advanced technical aspects of this complex area of the game are beyond the limitations of this introductory water polo skills guide.

Communication

Communication has been frequently mentioned throughout this book, but it is critical to reiterate that players should constantly communicate with each by calling out, signaling and using non-verbal cues to one another across all phases of the game.

Communication between players is often heard in the form of verbal calls, giving directions to teammates and alerting each other to threats when in defense, and opportunities when on offense. However, non-verbal communication also plays a vital role trough hand gestures, a nod of the head or even a wink. The goalkeeper also has a role in this respect, and information coming from the coaching bench is also a very common form of communication throughout a water polo match.

Summary

There are many other tricks and tips that can be programmed and performed in water polo, but the techniques outlined in this chapter are more commonly used by competent and experienced water polo players. After these various skills have been introduced, practiced and mastered, they will enhance the effectiveness of players across all levels of the game.

This book has attempted to merge the delivery of knowledge in the form of instructions through written text with the demonstrative imagery of photography to strengthen the learning of water polo skills. It is important to remember that 'How to Play Water Polo' is intended for athletes in the beginning and intermediate stages of skill development.

In studying these 11 chapters and associated sections, learners have been exposed to 68 separate skills, 21 different types of shots, and a further 30 water polo tips and tricks that are mostly essential for effectively competing and playing the game of water polo. I sincerely hope that you have improved your knowledge and skills, and wish you the very best of success in the future with our great game.

'The bronze medal match between Greece (winners) and Italy (blue caps) at the 16th FINA World Championships, Kazan, Russia', by Oleg Bkhambri (Voltmetro), (8 Aug 2015). [See p. 211].

Checklist of Water Polo Tips & Tricks

Skill #	Skill Name	✔	Date Mastered
64	Competing in the Water		
65	Defensive Phase Tips		
a	*Passing Lanes*		
b	*Ball Under*		
c	*No Fouls*		
d	*Pressure*		
e	*Push Out*		
f	*Overpower*		
g	*Hinder*		
h	*Never Assist*		
i	*Swimsuit Hold*		
66	Swimming Phase Tips		
a	*Keep Moving*		
b	*Ball Side*		
c	*Stop & Start*		
d	*Push Assist*		
e	*Underarm Slide*		
f	*Acting Foul*		
g	*Hip Swim*		
h	*Arm Check & Go*		
67	Offensive Phase Tips		
a	*Give & Go*		
b	*Selfie Free Throw*		
c	*Leg Fend*		
d	*90⁰ Turn Out*		
e	*Twister*		
f	*Pull Through*		
g	*Centre-Back Flick*		
68	Goalkeeper Tips		
a	*Offset Save*		
b	*Pick A Side*		
c	*Watch The Eyes*		
d	*Jamming Down*		
e	*Lob Save*		
f	*Ball Steal*		

'Water Polo at Athens Olympic Aquatic Centre',
by Vchristos, (Aug 2004). [See p. 211].

APPENDICES

A. GLOSSARY

Numbers 0-9

2 meter defense - See hole D.

2 meter line - The line at each end of the pool crossing 2 meters in front of the goal, designated by a red mark on the edge of the pool. The edge of the playing area from the 2 meter mark to the goal line is a red line.

2 meter offense - See center forward.

2 meter zone or area - The area between the 2 meter line and the goal line. No attacking player may be in this area without the ball.

2 on 1 attack. A numerical advantage in the offensive phase.

3-3 offense - A basic positional offense composed of two lines containing 3 players each: point and two drivers along the 5 meter line, and wings and center forward along the 2 meter line.

3 on 2 attack. A numerical advantage in the offensive phase.

4 meter line (obsolete) - Prior to FINA rule changes in 2005, this was the position for penalty throws, replaced by the present 5 meter line.

4-2 extra-man offense - Team on offense positions four players on the 2 meter line, and two players on 5 meter line. Commonly used in man up situations.

5 meter line - The line at each end of the pool crossing 5 meters in front of the goal, designated by a yellow mark on the edge of the pool. The edge of the pool from the 5 meter mark to the 2 meter mark is a yellow line. A player may shoot at the goal from beyond this line without taking a free pass after an ordinary foul, if the shot is made with one continuous motion.

5 meter shot - See penalty shot.

6 on 5 offense - See man-up.

A

advantage rule - The referee may refrain from calling a foul if it would give an advantage to the offending player's team.

angle - cutting the angle: The path that a defender must swim to cut off a fast breaking attacker. [2] *goal angle:* The triangle between the ball carrier and the two goal posts. The goalkeeper must play the angle, or position himself to best contest the shot.

assist - A pass to a teammate that leads directly to scoring a goal.

attacker - A field player on the team in possession of the ball; see Offense (sports).

B

back door - Offensive player on the weak side gets behind his defender and open for a quick shot.

backhand - A pass or shot in which the ball carrier flips the ball directly behind him.

ball - A water polo ball is usually a bright yellow color with a gripable surface, allowing it to be held with one hand despite its large size. The cover is a buffed rubberized fabric over a wound nylon fiber base with an inflatable bladder. Ball weight is 400-450 grams (14-16 ounces) and inflated to approximately 90 kPa (13 PSI) of pressure. Water polo balls come in two main sizes: size 5 (0.7 meters or 28 inches in circumference), intended for use by men, and size 4 (0.65 meters or 26.5 inches in circumference), intended for women.

ball out - The referee calls for the ball to be thrown to him during a timeout or dead time.

ball under - The player holding the ball, if it is forced under water as a result of contact with a defender, is charged with an ordinary foul, and loses possession.

baulk - See pump fake.

bat shot - See t shot.

blue ball - Shouted to teammates when dark cap team has possession.

bounce shot - See skip shot.

box out - As a shot or pass is taken, a player moves quickly in front of the opponent to prevent the opponent from recovering the pass or rebound.

breakaway - See fast break.

brutality - A violent foul with intention to harm. The fouling player is ejected from the game without substitution. The opponents are awarded a penalty shot, and the ejected player's team plays one man down for the next four minutes of game time. This type of foul is signaled by the referee by crossing the arms in the form of an X.

bunny - A goal scored on a power shot close to the goalkeepers head.

C

caps - Visiting team field players wear numbered white caps, and home team field players wear dark caps. Both starting goalkeepers wear quartered red caps, numbered "1", substitute goalies caps are numbered either "1-A" in NCAA play or "13" for FINA international play. Caps are fitted with ear protectors.

center forward - Offense player positioned at the 2 meter line in front of the opposing team's goal. Also called 2 meter offense or hole set.

check - To place a hand or forearm on an opponent's chest to hinder movement or maintain position. Also called chug.

cherry picking - A player stays on his offensive end of the pool when the rest of his team is defending, waiting for a turnover, often resulting in a long pass and uncontested goal.

commit - To make a move or take a position over other options, from which recovery is difficult.

corner throw - Free throw awarded to the attacking team when the ball is deflected over the goal line and out of the playing area by the goalkeeper (but NOT defending field player). An attacker puts the ball in play from the 2 meter mark at the edge of the pool.

counter-attack, counter - Transition when the defensive team regains control of the ball, advances the ball and sets up offense in front of the opponent's goal.

cover back - Call to defensive teammates to defend players between them and their goal.

crash back - All six defensive field players swim back rapidly to the center of their end as soon as the other team recovers possession, to counter the offensive counter-attack.

D

dead time - The time between the whistle for a foul and the restarting of play and the clock. A foul during dead time results in a player ejection. See free throw.

donut - A goal scored over the goalie's outstretched arms.

double post - Offense with two attackers on the 2 meter line in front of the opponent's goal. Also called double hole.

draw a foul (ejection) - Causing an opponent to receive a foul (or ejection).

dribbling - The technique of moving the ball while swimming forward, propelled ahead of the player with the wake created by alternating arm-strokes. Since ball contact is minimal, this creates advantage for the ball carrier advancing the ball; his defender may not make contact unless the attacker is touching the ball.

driver - A perimeter player in the 3-3 offense, positioned on either side of the point or center forward, who attempts to swim toward the goal to escape his defender, receive the ball and score.

drop - Defenders swim back to the center of the pool to block passes and shots by advancing attackers, while a defender presses the ball carrier to cause a hurried pass.

dry pass - A pass thrown and caught on one hand between players; the ball does not touch the water. This pass allows for optimal speed due to fluid motion between catching and throwing.

dumping the ball - An attacking player throws the ball into a far corner, away from the defenders, before the 30 seconds of possession expires for his team, to avoid a fast break opportunity for the opposing team.

E

egg-beater - A form of treading water, named because the circular movement of the legs resembles the motion of an egg-beater. This kick allows the player to maintain a constant position to the water level, and also by kicking faster for a brief period the player can get high out of the water for a block, pass, or shot.

ejection - See exclusion foul.

entry pass - Also called entering the ball, refers to the pass, most often a wet pass, into the center forward or 2-meter man. Most offenses focus on entering the ball early in the shot clock, and reacting if a foul or ejection is drawn.

extra-man - See man-up.

F

face off - See neutral throw.

fast break - The team recovering the ball, usually after an unexpected turnover, sprints to the opponent's goal to gain an advantage in numbers or position, and an easy goal.

field player - One of a team's six players who swim up and down the field of play, excluding the goalkeeper.

FINA - Federation Internationale de Natation, the international organization governing water polo (and swimming) competitions and rules.

flat - An offensive player position, on either side of the point, about 5 to 8 meters out from the goal. See also driver.

fouls - Very common in water polo, both as a defensive strategy or because of holding (usually underwater) and rough play.
  • Ordinary or minor foul: The

referee signals with one short whistle blow and points one hand to the spot of the foul and the other hand in the direction of the team who gains possession. Play continues immediately.

- If by a defender preventing the free movement of an opponent who is not holding the ball, the attacking team has a free throw. The player fouled has three seconds to make a free pass to another offensive player.
- If the attacking team delays play, allows the ball to be pushed underwater, has a player inside the two meter area without the ball or pushes a defending player to create space for a pass or shot, the opposing team is given possession of the ball and play resumes immediately.
- Exclusion or major foul: A referee signals a major foul by two short whistle bursts and indicates that the player must leave the field without impacting play and move to the penalty area for twenty seconds.
- Dunking (sinking in FINA rules), intentional splashing, or pulling an opponent back who does not have the ball, also interfering with a free throw or attempting to block a shot with two hands.
- Striking another player intentionally, misconduct or disrespect will also result in exclusion for the entire game.
- Penalty foul: The referee signals by blowing his whistle and raising five fingers.
- Any foul is committed inside the 5-meter line and the offensive player had an opportunity to score, or a goal was prevented by the foul. A penalty shot is awarded from the five meter line.
- Exclusion and penalties fouls are called personal fouls. A player who receives three personal fouls must sit out the remainder of the match.

free throw - After an ordinary foul, a player of the team retaining possession of the ball puts the ball in play without delay. The defender may not challenge the player in possession until the ball leaves his hand. After a foul, the player putting the ball in play may only make a direct shot on goal if he is beyond the 5 meter line and shoots with one continuous motion.

front - Defensive tactic by the hole D when guarding the center forward close to the 2 meter line. The hole D moves between the center forward and the ball to cut off the passing lane.

G

gamed - A player is "gamed" who receives a third exclusion foul or is removed from play for misconduct and may not return for the remainder of the game.

give and go - Offensive move where player passes the ball and then drives toward the goal to receive a pass and attempt a shot.

goal - Refers to both the result of a score and the physical structure that defines where a score is achieved. A goal is scored after the ball passes completely over the goal line, between the goal posts and under the crossbar. The goal posts are 3 meters apart and the crossbar is 0.9 meters above the water surface.

goal line - The line at each end of the pool crossing the front of the goal, designated by a white mark on the edge of the pool. The playing area extends 0.3 meters behind the goal line, which must be at least 1.66 meters from the pool wall.

goal judge - Official positioned at each goal line who rules on entry of players, goal scoring, corner and penalty throws, and the start of play.

goalkeeper or goalie - The player for each team assigned to remain directly in front of the goal to prevent the opposite team from scoring. Within the five meter area in front of his goal, the goalkeeper may touch the ball with two hands, strike the ball with a clenched fist and touch the bottom of the pool (depth permitting). Unlike the field players, he cannot cross the half-distance line. Both goalkeepers wear quartered red caps, numbered "1".

goal throw - A free pass by the defending goalkeeper from behind the 2 meter line to restart play, if anyone but the defending goalkeeper was last to touch the ball before it went out over the goal line.

greenie - A quick shot taken by a perimeter player following a pass from the hole set. Derived from guerrini.

H

half-distance line - The midpoint of the pool or playing area, designated on the pool edge by a white mark. The ball is dropped here at the start of play. The edge of the playing area from the half-distance line to each 5 meter line is marked with a green line.

hole - Position directly in front of the goal, closest to the 2 meter line.

hole D - Defense player or position on the 2 meter line directly in front of the goal. This position is also called 2 meter defense or hole guard.

hole set - Offense player or position on the 2 meter line directly in front of the goal. This position is also called 2 meter offense or center forward.

I

impede - Defensive guarding that prevents a player from moving; a foul if the impeded player does not have the ball.

inner tube water polo - A version of water polo in which players are allowed to float in inner tubes to avoid treading water during the game, which requires superb conditioning. Usually played as an intramural sport on college campuses, often coed.

inside water - Best position for a defender: between the attacker he is guarding and the goal.

inside water shot - The shooter swims toward the goal and unexpectedly flips the ball out of the water past the goalkeeper into the goal, timed with his swimming stroke. Examples are the pop shot and spring shot.

J

Jam - Defenders crash back and occupy the center of the pool, forcing any fast break to the outside and toward the perimeter positions. See drop.

K

kickout (KO) - See fouls-exclusion foul.

L

lane press - Defenders closely guard the player with the ball and attempt to block the passing lanes.

lead - To throw a pass ahead of a teammate who is swimming.

loading the ball - To transfer the ball from one hand to the other immediately before a shot, often misdirecting the goalkeeper and increasing the speed and suddenness of the shot.

lob shot - An outside water shot thrown with a high arc, intended to pass over the goalie's hands and under the crossbar.

M

man to man - Defensive tactic where each attacker is guarded by a specific defender, regardless of his position on the field of play.

man up - A team has one player more than its opponent, after a player of the opposing team is ejected for an exclusion foul.

math- A tactical approach to winning games.

N

natural goal - A goal scored from play with both teams at full strength, i.e., not a man up or penalty throw.

neutral throw - The referee restarts play by throwing the ball into the pool between two opposing players, giving each an equal opportunity to recover the ball (like a jump ball in basketball). A neutral throw results when players of each team commit a fouls at the same time, or if the referees disagree on which team committed a foul.

no set - A call from the goalie or point to his offensive teammates to avoid passing the ball into the hole set because of close coverage by defenders. See setting the ball.

O

open - When an offensive player is not guarded by a defender.

outlet pass - During the counter-attack, the goalkeeper looks to pass to an open teammate down field who is fast breaking to the goal or setting up the offense.

outside water shot - The shooter holds the ball out of water before taking the shot at the goal, i.e.: power shot, lob shot or skip shot. Outside water shots require a player to stop swimming, and usually occur outside the 2 meter zone.

overplay - A player commits too early and is caught out of position by an opponent's move.

overtime - If the score is tied at the end of regulation play, two overtime periods of three minutes each are played. Overtime periods are common in tournament

play due to the high level of skill of these superior teams.

P

pants - An optional addition.

pass - see dry pass and wet pass.

passing lane - The path between the player with the ball and his teammate to whom he intends to pass.

period - The game is divided into four periods; the length depends on the level of play (Int. - 8 min of stoppage time per quarter, but less for beginners).

penalty shootout - A tie breaker if the score is tied after two overtime periods. Five players and a goalkeeper are chosen by the coaches of each team. Players shoot from the 5-meter line alternately at either end of the pool in turn until all five have taken a shot. If the score is still tied, the same players shoot alternately until one team misses and the other scores, deciding the winner.

penalty shot - See penalty throw.

penalty throw - A shot awarded when any foul is committed inside the five meter line and the offensive player had an opportunity to score, or a goal was prevented by the foul. The penalty shot is attempted from five meters with play stopped. Any defenders flanking the player taking the shot must be no closer than two meters. The goalkeeper must be on the goal line. The referee signals with a whistle and by lowering his arm, and the player taking the penalty shot must immediately throw the ball with an uninterrupted motion toward the goal.

perimeter player - The five offensive positions, other than the center forward, i.e.: wings, drivers and point. The perimeter players interchange their positions several times during a single offensive play.

point - Position on offense in the center of the line furthest from the goal. The point player's position provides opportunities to pass to teammates and communicate among the offense, like the point guard in basketball.

pop shot - An inside water shot, executed by scooping the ball with the non-dominant hand, and "popping" the ball upward, as the player treads up out of the water to meet the ball at its highest point with his/her outstretched dominant hand and shoots at the goal. During the flight of the ball, from when it is "Popped" up until it reaches the shooting-hand, and contact from behind by a defender will result in a 5-meter penalty shot, and thus it is an effective tool when one has inside water.

possession - Undisputed control of the ball. The team with the ball has 30 seconds to take a shot until possession is given to the opposing team.

power play - See man up.

power shot - An outside water shot in which a player propels his body out of the water and uses his momentum to shoot the ball into the net.

press - Defensive pressure on the attacking team by closely defending each player man to man. See also lane press.

pump fake - When using an outside water shot, the player gets in position to shoot and but stops halfway through, immobilizing or misdirecting the goalkeeper before releasing the ball.

Q

quarter - See period.

R

Rear-back - a move used by an attacking player to create space between him/herself and their defender in an attempt to become open for a pass and subsequently attempt a shot. The attacker begins to swim toward the opponents' goal and abruptly stops and slides backward, awaiting a pass from a teammate, usually the center or 2-meter man.

rebound - After an unsuccessful shot at the goal, the ball becomes free in the water, and can be recovered by the offense for another goal attempt or by the defense for a counter-attack. A rebound after a shot on goal resets the 30 second possession clock.

red - Shouted to teammates when 10 seconds remain on the shot clock, or in cases where a different color (usually yellow) is used to signify 10 seconds, red can be used to warn teammates of only 5 seconds remaining on the shot clock.

red card - Shown by a referee to signify that a coach, substitute, or bench personnel has been excluded for misconduct, and is required to leave the pool area immediately and cannot return to the game. See also yellow card.

red flag - A red flag is used by officials at the scorer/timekeeper's table to signal when a player has received three exclusion fouls and must sit out the rest of the game.

re-entry area - Area at each end of the pool near each team bench, designated by a red line, where players may enter and exit the playing area for substitution or exclusion penalties.

referee - The two referees control the players, game play and the playing area throughout the match. Their decisions are final including rule infractions, fouls, scoring, possession of the ball and rulings of the timekeeper and goal judges. One referee stands on each side of the pool. The referee with the goal to his right when a team is on the attack is called the attacking or offensive referee. The other, the defensive referee, remains as far back as the attacking player who is furthest from the goal. When the other team regains the ball, their roles reverse as the ball moves to the other goal.

release - To break free from a defender to receive a pass.

rolled - the foul regarding a misconduct or game exclusion. This is because of the referee's circular arm motions signifying the player is done for the game.

S

save - Successful blocked shot by the goalkeeper. Also called a stop.

setting a screen (or pick) - An offense player is positioned to allow his teammate to swim by, while blocking or delaying his defender.

setting the ball - To pass the ball into the center forward, ideally just out of reach of his defender, allowing the center to lunge for the ball and sweep it into the goal with a backhand or power shot.

shot clock - A clock at each corner of the pool deck counting down (from 30 seconds) the time remaining for a team to take a shot. Also known as the possession clock.

sink - To push an opposing player under the water, an exclusion foul if the player is not holding the ball and is in a position of offensive advantage.

skip shot - An outside water shot executed by throwing the ball at an angle directly into the water. If done properly and with enough force, the ball will skip off the water into the goal, since the goalkeeper cannot easily anticipate the angle. Also called a bounce shot.

slough - A defensive perimeter player intentionally causes an ordinary foul and then moves toward the goal, away from his attacker, who must take a free throw. This tactic allows the defense an opportunity to double-team the hole set and possibly steal the inbound pass. Also called foul and in or foul and drop.

spring shot - An inside water shot executed by pushing the ball slightly into the water (but avoiding a ball under foul) and then allowing a sudden release, and a soft tap-in to beat the goalkeeper.

sprint - At the start of each period, teams line up on their own goal line. At the referee's whistle, both teams swim to midpoint of the field, where the referee drops the ball. The first team to recover the ball begins their offense.

stalling - Failing to take a shot within 30 seconds or intentional delay in advancing the ball results in a turnover.

swim off - See sprint.

switch - Players change defensive assignments to cover a teammate who has fallen behind an opponent, or to match up better with an offensive player in size or speed.

T

tee shot - Executed by scooping the ball with the non-dominant hand, loading the ball to the dominant hand, and propelling the ball forward. The off-hand sets itself up as a tee, as in golf or baseball, and the two hands also finish in the shape of a "T".

timeout - Each team may call two 60 second

timeouts in the four periods of regulation play, and one timeout if the game goes into overtime. During game play, only the team in possession of the ball may call a timeout.

tube water polo - See inner tube water polo

turn a defender - An offensive move to get by an opponent using leverage or strength. The result is a 180 degree turn, where the defender is "wheeled" around, resulting in the attacking player possessing inside-water, or position towards the goal, with the defender trailing behind. This maneuver often results in the defender being forced to foul.

turnover - A team loses possession of the ball, which reverts to the opponent, as a result of a foul or possession for more than 30 seconds without a shot on goal.

U

utility player - A player skilled at several offensive or defensive roles, often coming off the bench for substitutions.

USA Water Polo - The National Governing Body (NGB) for the sport of water polo in the United States.

V

V-cut - Offensive player cuts in and quickly out of the defender's area, pushing off of the defender to increase speed; making the letter "V". Also called "V-out".

W

walk it in - The attacker grips the ball in one hand and either eggbeaters or strokes in toward the goal.

weak side - When an offensive player has possession of the ball on one side of the playing area (the strong side), the

opposite side is called the weak side. Players will shout "weak" to notify a teammate with the ball that they are open on the other side of the pool.

wet pass - A deliberate pass into the water, just out of reach of the intended teammate and their defender. The receiving player can then lunge towards the ball and out of the water to make a shot or pass.

white ball - Shouted to teammates when white cap team has possession.

wing - The position on offense on either side of the center forward, along the 2 meter line. Players at this position may set screens for the drivers, recover rebounds, and shift laterally or toward the half-distance line to spread out the defenders. More generally, the wing is a player or location to either side of the center of the playing area. To move toward the side of the pool to get open for a pass is to wing out.

Y

yellow card - Shown by the referee to indicate that a coach, substitute, or bench personnel has been officially cautioned for misconduct, but may continue participating in the game. If a person receives a second yellow card caution, it has the effect of receiving a red card, and the individual must leave the playing area for the rest of the match. Players in the water are not show yellow card in Water Polo.

Z

zone - Defensive arrangement in which players are assigned to defend an area, rather than a specific opponent.

'The bronze medal water polo match at the 16th World Championships, between Greece and Italy in Kazan Russia', by Oleg Bkhambri (Voltmetro), (8 Aug 2015). [See p. 213].

B. IMAGE ATTRIBUTIONS

Front Cover - 'DFC Sète's Dražen Kujačić prepares to throw the ball in their quarter-final against FNC Douai of the 2014 League Cup at the Georges Vallerey swimming pool in Paris', by Marie-Lan Nguyen (15 March 2014). Available at [https://commons.wikimedia.org/wiki/File:DFC_Sete_v_FNC_Douai_Coupe_de_la_Ligue_2014_t140138.jpg] under the Creative Commons Attribution 3.0 Unported license. Full terms at http://creativecommons.org/licenses/2.0.

Page 2 - 'Women's Water Polo team at practice [#129]', by Sean Fornelli, (2008). Available at [https://www.flickr.com/photos/seaners4real/2723929883/in/photolist-59GRsk-59CRRe-59BdrT-59FXM1-59Gc3b-59Cq4P-59FyCG-59G9ZN-59CmTa-59CiJ2-59BeVt-59GaZu-59GJBz-59G36b-59FnHA-fprE5y-59BG4B-59GGNB-59DbTT-59BobH-59GHPG-59Ceqp-59C7CR-59DrJV-59H2Kb-59FHCb-59Ger7-fprAN5-59FLDU-59Bpp2-59HCSC-59GWB1-59GgCE-59CddP-59GEqD-59ChFF-59GyfQ-59CK5c-59GiKb-59LYZy-59H9ho-59GPYR-59Cxv6-59GSBs-59GFX8-59CMap-59GEJW-cLrt5G-59GM91-59GsYJ] under a Creative Commons Attribution - ShareAlike 2.0 Generic. Full terms at http://creativecommons.org/licenses/by/2.0.

Chapter 1

Due to the expiration of copyright - all images used in Chapter 1 are in the Public Domain.

Chapter 2

Page 37 - 'Australia vs Kazahstan at London Olympic Games', by Matt Brown, (31 July 2012). Available at [https://commons.wikimedia.org/wiki/File:Inside_the_polo_arena_-_2012_Olympics.jpg] under a Creative Commons Attribution - 2.0 Generic. Full terms at http://creativecommons.org/licenses/by/2.0.

Page 39 - 'Italian water polo match - C.N.Salerno vs Pro Recco', by Di Iorio Gabriele, (undated). Available at [https://upload.wikimedia.org/wikipedia/it/1/1e/Di_Iorio_Gabriele.jpg] and is in the Public Domain by permission of the Author

Page 47 - Attribution - unknown. Licensed under a Creative Commons Attribution - ShareAlike 2.0 Generic. Full terms at http://creativecommons.org/licenses/by/2.0.

Page 49 - Attribution - unknown. Licensed under a Creative Commons Attribution - ShareAlike 2.0 Generic. Full terms at http://creativecommons.org/licenses/by/2.0.

Page 50 - Attribution - unknown. Licensed under a Creative Commons Attribution - ShareAlike 2.0 Generic. Full terms at http://creativecommons.org/licenses/by/2.0.

Chapter 3

Page 51 - 'George French (CLU) and Ryan Warde (UCI) play in the UC Irvine vs Cal Lutheran match, score 11-5', by Chris Hunkeler, (2 Sep 2016). Available at [https://www.flickr.com/photos/chrishunkeler/32147416031] under a Creative Commons Attribution - 2.0 Generic. Full terms at http://creativecommons.org/licenses/by/2.0.

Page 55 - Attribution - unknown. Licensed under a Creative Commons Attribution -

ShareAlike 2.0 Generic. Full terms at http://creativecommons.org/licenses/by/2.0.

Page 62 - Attribution - unknown. Licensed under a Creative Commons Attribution - ShareAlike 2.0 Generic. Full terms at http://creativecommons.org/licenses/by/2.0.

Page 64 - 'Jumping out with great egg-beater kick by Sofia Konuch of Russia [Русский: Конух Софья Евгеньевна]', by Quelle: Eigenes Werk; ShaMan186, (4 Aug 2017). Available at [https://upload.wikimedia.org/wikipedia/commons/7/75/Konuch.png] under a Creative Commons Attribution - 4.0 International. Full terms at http://creativecommons.org/licenses/by/2.0.

Chapter 4

Page 67 - Attribution - unknown. Licensed under a Creative Commons Attribution - ShareAlike 2.0 Generic. Full terms at http://creativecommons.org/licenses/by/2.0.

Page 74 - 'Women's Water Polo team at practice [#062]', by Sean Fornelli, (31 July 2008). Available at [https://www.flickr.com/photos/seaners4real/2723053319/in/photolist-59CmTa-59CiJ2-59BMtR-59FFbq-59FpfC-59FzF1-59C5rH-59GJBz-59FnHA-59FMw3-59Cp1F-59BG4B-59GGNB-59DbTT-59BobH-59GHPG-59DrJV-59FP77-59BVNi-59FHCb-59FRSC-59HFW1-59Bpp2-59GDCc-59HCSC-59GWB1-59GgCE-59GTEw-59GDGf-59LZQb-59CddP-59GEqD-59Ceqp-59CH5k-59ChFF-59BQPH-59GsYJ-59HwME-59Cxv6-Rbe6Ag-R7PPYj-QAXVE7-PTSoUQ-R7PRKW-R7PFr9-QPz3Y4-QPz4Rg-QX37Fj-59GyfQ-59CK5c] under a Creative Commons Attribution - ShareAlike 2.0 Generic. Full terms at http://creativecommons.org/licenses/by/2.0.

Page 77 - 'George French (CLU) plays in the Air Force vs Cal Lutheran match, score 14-8', by Chris Hunkeler, (2 Sep 2106). Available at [https://www.flickr.com/photos/chrishunkeler/32035535911/in/photolist-QNSuJ4-QqXViq-GEwvpb-23EfUgn-PNJWMy-23EfTNt-23WCcpS-23WCc41-223kCvw-23EfTe2-PSmL9i-R7PFr9-GEwuWY-23WCd3f-23EfSKB-R66rwV-23EfV18-23WCcDu--223kEMs-23EfSrk-GjCta9-23EfTWz-23EfTbM-23EfTfe-23EfUJr-23EfSwk-23EfUNV-223kCCC-223kBJo-23EfUkF-24Nit92-23EfTHD-23rccgv-223kFkm-23WCc2h-GEwssj-23EfUeP-FneQrT-FneQzP-23WCcFU-QYKUMD-23EfUpP-223kBYm-223kCvo-23WCcyQ-23WCcWJ-23EfURv-23EfTRz-23EfTCZ-24Nirkn] under a Creative Commons Attribution - 2.0 Generic. Full terms at http://creativecommons.org/licenses/by/2.0.

Chapter 5

Page 81 - Attribution - unknown. Licensed under a Creative Commons Attribution - ShareAlike 2.0 Generic. Full terms at http://creativecommons.org/licenses/by/2.0.

Page 85 - 'Water polo player - Kyriakos Pontikeas, Olympiakos, Greece', by by Kallipon, (30 May 2016). Available at [https://pt.m.wikipedia.org/wiki/Kyriakos_Pontikeas#/media/Ficheiro%3AOΣΘΠ.jpg] under a Creative Commons Attribution - ShareAlike 4.0 Generic. Full terms at http://creativecommons.org/licenses/by/2.0.

Page 88 - 'Zac Polmanteer (Redlands) and Riley Smith (LMU) play in the Loyola Marymount vs Redlands match, score 12-11', by Chris Hunkeler, (2 Sep 2016).

Available at [https://www.flickr.com/photos/chrishunkeler/31766546680] under a Creative Commons Attribution - 2.0 Generic. Full terms at http://creativecommons.org/licenses/by/2.0.

Page 89 (top) - 'Dayne Jagga (LMU) plays in the Loyola Marymount vs Redlands match, score 12-11', by Chris Hunkeler, (2 Sep 2016). Available at [https://www.flickr.com/photos/chrishunkeler/32141624155/in/photolist-dhLq8d-7hGKJP-PNJF49-QK7C77-QYfe4H-QUzQJc-PRuppx-PSmEHt-PSmL9i] under a Creative Commons Attribution - 2.0 Generic. Full terms at http://creativecommons.org/licenses/by/2.0

Page 89 (bottom) - 'Water polo player from LHS, USA looking to throw a dry pass', by Pexels, (2015). Available at [https://www.pexels.com/photo/water-polo-175852/] under a Creative Commons Attribution - Zero (CC0) License. Full terms at http://creativecommons.org/licenses/by/2.0.

Page 94 - 'Water polo player rolling over to perform a roll out pass [20130924-DSC_7477.jpg]', by jj_mom, (24 Sep 2013). Available at [https://www.flickr.com/photos/25142250@N02/9976114145/in/photolist-gcycb2-9yzzHj-6WNMWj-dstS87-raVZJ7-8YkN1X-dy56wa-9ywUuD-fprAN5-6WJQuD-9ywL4F-59FWEy-aAkE2q-fNSv1q-9ywM1c-2EPmR-6WJSWT-nckinp-59BdrT-6sx2o9-dyayo9-59Hagb-aAFQG9-aNRREM-9yzueQ-9ywTZe-59CRRe-aAFR1u-9yzzHN-8spPrc-dE769-5eePjR-dxQUPb-8zT6Ad-9ywWzF-9ywJYt-7LWSUy-q9XuyE-dyaAaW-jdqSK7-dy58kc-59FXM1-8MBR1X-jdoNQi-9ywQZ8-bWThFB-aAD7tv-ecnbcP-59Cq4P-jdoLp6] under a Creative Commons Attribution - ShareAlike 2.0 Generic. Full terms at http://creativecommons.org/licenses/by/2.0.

Page 97 - 'Francesco Di Fulvio, Pro Recco', by Roberto Faccenda, (12 Nov, 2016). Available at [https://www.flickr.com/photos/stefanedberg62/30905455750] under a Creative Commons Attribution - ShareAlike 2.0 Generic. Full terms at http://creativecommons.org/licenses/by/2.0.

Chapter 6

Page 99 - 'Women's Water Polo team at practice [#054]', by Sean Fornelli, (2008). Available at [https://www.flickr.com/photos/seaners4real/2723024183/in/photolist-59CddP-59GEqD-59ChFF-59GyfQ-59CK5c-59GiKb-59LYZy-59H9ho-59GPYR-59Cxv6-59GSBs-59GFX8-59CMap-59GEJW-cLrt5G-59GM91-59GsYJ-23NCLe8-59GNaH-59Dmfi-59HuNd-59BtYe-59Hbfu-59G7ZL-59BMtR-59Dpek-59C5rH-59FMw3-59FYM3-59Hd8Y-59FRSC-59GDCc-59BwAX-59GDGf-59LZQb-59DkfF-59CaYR-59HwME-59HH1b-59GpuY-59HESG-59GYWf-59CYue-59HrKY-Kt3Hx-59Gu4C-59H3FQ-59Df3K-25aJjLp-NNszQf] under a Creative Commons Attribution - ShareAlike 2.0 Generic. Full terms at http://creativecommons.org/licenses/by/2.0.

Page 105 - 'With the score tied 1-1 in the first quarter of the game, Stephen Siri drives the ball to Matt Burton around Air Force defense. Siri had a total of three assists in the game. Air Force was able to draw a lot of ejections off of USC, making the Trojans play a man down and giving Air Force a 6 on 5 man advantage in the beginning of the game', by Neon Tommy, (1 Dec 2012). Available at [https://www.flickr.com/photos/neontommy/8235571217/in/photolist-dxKspc-6xZH7t-6xZtG6-6xZP8R-6y4Vp7-9H572c-9H7yzN-9H7Zoq-9H57hR-9H7ZJo-9H7XMJ-9H56WT-6xZBBB-6xZyKZ-8yK4cf-6xZw3k-cAB4dW-6xZEWR-cACusN-

6xZqVX-cAB54y-f5gitD-6xZJnV-22i5Se-f5vyAQ-RLjPBh-6y4CtE-7ZRoR5-HE4xZL-f5gnHi-RtJv4e-RauRDh-R3zziu-QwLmty-R6X6zk-QVtc62-QK7C77-PHJLrJ-Qp6QGN-QLcmbU-Qp6RAG-QqXWGC-QNStSK-Q2XWgP-QSNnyh-QUAeae-QVtzTr-QqXY3J-QPDsgi-PNJB33] under a Creative Commons Attribution - 2.0 Generic. Full terms at http://creativecommons.org/licenses/by/2.0.

Page 109 - 'Greece vs Hungary Water Polo match at the World Junior Championship, Naples, Italy, 2004', by Massimo Finizio, (2004). Available at [https://upload.wikimedia.org/wikipedia/commons/e/e5/WaterPolo.JPG] under a Creative Commons Attribution - ShareAlike 2.0 Generic. Full terms at http://creativecommons.org/licenses/by/2.0.

Chapter 7

Page 111 - 'Rio de Janeiro - Seleção masculina brasileira de polo aquático vence a da Sérvia por 6 a 5 nos Jogos Olímpicos Rio 2016, no Parque Aquático Maria Lenk', by Fernando Frazão/Agência Brasil, Agência Brasil Fotografias, (10 Aug 2016). Available at [https://no.wikipedia.org/wiki/Gustavo_Guimarães#/media/File:Gustavo_Guimarães_Rio_2016.jpg] under a Creative Commons Attribution - 2.0 Generic. Full terms at http://creativecommons.org/licenses/by/2.0.

Page 115 - 'Edward Moss (LMU) and Luke Ritter (LB) play in the Long Beach State vs Loyola Marymount match, score 11-7', by Chris Hunkeler, (2 Sep 2016). Available at [https://www.flickr.com/photos/chrishunkeler/31843173150] under a Creative Commons Attribution - 2.0 Generic. Full terms at http://creativecommons.org/licenses/by/2.0.

Page 116 - 'Frame extracted from miniDV movie taken May 2005 at a boys high school water polo match', by Ryanjo, (16 Apr 2006). Available at [https://upload.wikimedia.org/wikipedia/en/0/05/Water_Polo_Eggbeater.jpg] under a Creative Commons Attribution - ShareAlike 3.0 Generic. Full terms at http://creativecommons.org/licenses/by/2.0.

Page 117 - 'Lee Griffin (LB) and Jon Beck (LMU) play in the Long Beach State vs Loyola Marymount match, score 11-7', by Chris Hunkeler, (2 Sep 2016). Available at [https://www.flickr.com/photos/chrishunkeler/31387838814/in/photolist-6xZqVX-cAB54y-f5gitD-6xZJnV-22i5Se-f5vyAQ-RLjPBh-6y4CtE-7ZRoR5-HE4xZL-f5gnHi-7wDRKq-qRoYLg-RtJv4e-RauRDh-R3zziu-QwLmty-R6X6zk-QVtc62-QK7C77-PHJLrJ-Qp6QGN-QLcmbU-XjyUUw-Qp6RAG-QqXWGC-QNStSK-Q2XWgP-QSNnyh-QUAeae-QVtzTr-QPDsgi-PNJB33-QYfe4H-PRukvR-PHJZz7-QUAiuB-R65XTZ-QqY1d5-R15FSR-QqY293-R3zyo3-PRtXfP-QUzQJc-QwL67m-PNJCkU-PHK3oo-QqXViq-PPCSWJ-7ZNeSB] under a Creative Commons Attribution - 2.0 Generic. Full terms at http://creativecommons.org/licenses/by/2.0.

Page 121 - The perfect tackle to stop a pass or shot. 'Iran men's national water polo team [#1]', by Ansari, (2016). Available at [https://upload.wikimedia.org/wikipedia/commons/4/44/Iran_men%27s_national_water_polo_team_3.jpg] under a Creative Commons Attribution - 4.0 International. Full terms at http://creativecommons.org/licenses/by/2.0.

Page 124 - 'Ilija Mustur - Montpellier Water Polo, France', by Roikiine, (20 Feb 2013). Available at [https://upload.wikimedia.org/wikipedia/commons/0/06/Montpellier-water-polo-ilija-mustur-roikiine.jpg] under a Creative Commons Attribution - ShareAlike 3.0 Generic. Full terms at http://creativecommons.org/licenses/by/2.0.

Page 126 (top) - 'Matteo Morelli (USC) and

Royce Daniel Laverne (CBU) play in the USC vs California Baptist match, score 16-3', by Chris Hunkeler, (2 Sep 2016). [See p.211]. Available at [https://www.flickr.com/photos/chrishunkeler/32044337501] under a Creative Commons Attribution - 2.0 Generic. Full terms at http://creativecommons.org/licenses/by/2.0.

Page 126 (bottom) - 'A spirited girls' high school water polo game in Central Florida in 2004', by Ryanjo, (posted 12 Apr 2006). Available at [https://en.wikipedia.org/wiki/File:Water_Polo_Defense.jpg] under a Creative Commons Attribution - ShareAlike 3.0 Generic. Full terms at http://creativecommons.org/licenses/by/2.0.

Chapter 8

Page 131 - COMCAM_130703-N-DY265-267 U.S. 5TH FLEET AREA OF RESPONSIBILITY U.S. Navy, Marine Corps and Army service members play water polo at Mina Salman Pier.' (U.S. Navy photo by Mass Communication Specialist 1st Class Mike Lenart/Released). Available at [https://www.flickr.com/photos/navcent/9240028652/in/photolist-cAB54y-f5gitD-6xZJnV-22i5Se-f5vyAQ-RLjPBh-6y4CtE-7ZRoR5-HE4xZL-f5gnHi-RtJv4e-RauRDh-R3zziu-QwLmty-R6X6zk-QVtc62-QK7C77-PHJLrJ-Qp6QGN-QLcmbU-Qp6RAG-QqXWGC-QNStSK-Q2XWgP-QSNnyh-QUAeae-QVtzTr-QqXY3J-QPDsgi-PNJB33-QYfe4H-PRukvR-PHJZz7-R65XTZ-QqY1d5-R15FSR-QqY293-R3zyo3-PRtXfP-QwL67m-PNJCkU-PHK3oo-QqXViq-PPCSWJ-7wDRKq-qRoYLg-XjyUUw-QUAiuB-QUzQJc-7ZNeSB] under a Creative Commons Attribution - 2.0 Generic. Full terms at http://creativecommons.org/licenses/by/2.0

Page 133 - 'A men's water polo exhibition game between the Pacific Tigers and Santa Clara Broncos at the Sullivan Aquatic Center in Santa Clara, California', by BrokenSphere, (18 July 2010). Available at [https://upload.wikimedia.org/wikipedia/commons/9/9c/Men%27s_water_polo_exhibition_game%2C_Pacific_at_Santa_Clara_2010-07-18_1.JPG] under the Creative Commons Attribution-Share Alike 3.0 Unported license.

Page 134 - 'Water Polo Sprint at the 2012 Summer Olympics', by Adam Russell, (2 Aug 2012). Available at [https://commons.wikimedia.org/wiki/File:Water_Polo_Sprint_(7773600758).jpg] under a Creative Commons Attribution - ShareAlike 2.0 Generic. Full terms at http://creativecommons.org/licenses/by/2.0.

Page 137 - 'MNE vs CRO on 2010 Men's European Water Polo Championship in Zagreb', byEx13, (2010). Available at [https://upload.wikimedia.org/wikipedia/commons/a/ac/MNE_vs_CRO_2010_Men%27s_European_Water_Polo_Championship.JPG] under a Creative Commons Attribution - ShareAlike 3.0 Generic. Full terms at http://creativecommons.org/licenses/by/2.0.

Page 138 - 'Womens Water Polo at the World Swimming Championships, Melbourne 2007 [#1]', by Flying Cloud, (2007). Available at [https://www.flickr.com/photos/flying_cloud/466828962] under a Creative Commons Attribution - ShareAlike 2.0 Generic. Full terms at http://creativecommons.org/licenses/by/2.0.

Page 140 - 'Womens Water Polo at the World Swimming Championships, Melbourne 2007 [#3]', by Flying Cloud, (2007). Available at [https://www.flickr.com/photos/flying_cloud/596666324/in/album-72157600441218707/] under a Creative Commons Attribution - ShareAlike 2.0 Generic. Full terms at http://creativecommons.org/licenses/by/2.0.

Attribution - unknown. Licensed under a Creative Commons Attribution - ShareAlike 2.0

Generic. Full terms at http://creativecommons.org/licenses/by/2.0.

Page 144 - 'Passing under pressure & looking for support', by Malcolm Slaney, (28 Oct 2017). Available at [https://www.flickr.com/photos/malcolmslaney/37950477686/] under a Creative Commons Attribution - 2.0 Generic. Full terms at http://creativecommons.org/licenses/by/2.0.

Page 145 - 'Iran men's national water polo team [#2]', by Ansari, (2016). Available at [https://upload.wikimedia.org/wikipedia/commons/9/92/Iran_men%27s_national_water_polo_team.jpg] under a Creative Commons Attribution - 4.0 International. Full terms at http://creativecommons.org/licenses/by/2.0.

Page 147 - 'The 5th test match at the AIS Aquatic Centre between Australia (white caps) women's national water polo team and Great Britain women's national water polo team. Australia won the test 14-3', by LauraHale, (28 Feb 2012). Available at [https://upload.wikimedia.org/wikipedia/commons/2/2e/Test_Five_AU_vs_GBR_0489.JPG] under a Creative Commons Attribution - ShareAlike 3.0 Generic. Full terms at http://creativecommons.org/licenses/by/2.0.

Page 149 - 'Eger vs Vasas water polo game at Eger, Hungary, by sikeri, (12 Apr 2014). Available at [https://www.flickr.com/photos/sikeri/13934901723/in/photolist-neo1Ng-nckkUU-nckfZP-fhJvoG-nckhZ1-nckaCB-nenVJP-dDG8M8-cMQ3eL-6xZH7t-9H7XZ3-6xZw3k-9H7Z9u-9H55N8-9H7Z5W-9H56Az-6xZP8R-6y4Vp7-9H572c-6xZqVX-9H7YzN-9H57hR-aAD9gg-6xZyKZ-9H7Zoq-9H7ZJo-aAD8cD-aAD7Wt-aAFTMG-9H7XMJ-6xZtG6-drLTVg-cEC6V1-drM2gJ-9H56WT-cAB4dW-6xZEWR-aAD8xR-aAD8p4-dxQURQ-6xZEB-B-cACusN-cAB54y-6xZJnV-aAFSAY-f5gitD-6y4CtE-dxKs5i-f5vyAQ-7ZRoR5] under a Creative Commons Attribution - 2.0 Generic. Full terms at http://creativecommons.org/licenses/by/2.0.

Chapter 9

Page 151 - 'Water polo shooter', by Ankarino, (18 Aug 2008). Available at [https://www.flickr.com/photos/ankarino/2776086696/] under a Creative Commons Attribution - ShareAlike 2.0 Generic. Full terms at http://creativecommons.org/licenses/by/2.0.

Page 153 - 'Partido de Waterpolo en Jaén, España [#2100]', by Juan Fernández, (2 Dec 2007). Available at [https://upload.wikimedia.org/wikipedia/commons/0/04/Water_polo-1.jpg] under a Creative Commons Attribution - ShareAlike 2.0 Generic. Full terms at http://creativecommons.org/licenses/by/2.0.

Page 154 - 'Water Polo shooter [3X9A4928]', by Malcolm Slaney, (undated). Available at [https://www.flickr.com/photos/malcolmslaney/28661193245/in/photolist-KEG7de-KxJZa8-KzZgTU-JGpA7P-JGkb3W-NFoMeo-KcJ965-JJesCt-JGnd8o-KvWKH6-2571XZW-KxLC7T-NNsAtu-JGqW4v-MTRp45-MTRpeW-KvgY7U-KxKWcc-JJ8WHQ-JJ9on5-MTRoTA-JGr2Fn-KcLL5L-KEHCFX-Kvhz9s-KEHnjK-JGn4ss-KCTh1R-KcKLxb-JJf8qD-NNsAV1-JJ9vHs-KA2DBu-22pMLNY-N4uq4U-NY8rvs-N4uq8S-2571XNd-MTRpty-22pMMa9-22pMLAJ-N4uqey-NR47Q7-NY8tfu-2571XTy-NFoLZL-22pMLDu-22pMLhs-2571XJ5-NY8tbG] under a Creative Commons Attribution - ShareAlike 2.0 Generic. Full terms at http://creativecommons.org/licenses/by/2.0.

Page 155 - Attribution - unknown. Licensed under a Creative Commons Attribution - ShareAlike 2.0 Generic. Full terms at http://creativecommons.org/licenses/by/2.0.

Page 159 - 'Brendan Fisher, water polo player takes a practice shot to warm up for the UC Irvine vs Cal Lutheran match', by Chris Hunkeler,

Once the skills in this book have been practiced and mastered, they will enhance the effectiveness of players across all ability levels of the game.

(2 Sep 2016). Available at [https://www.flickr.com/photos/chrishunkeler/31467025983] under a Creative Commons Attribution - ShareAlike 2.0 Generic. Full terms at http://creativecommons.org/licenses/by/2.0.

Page 160 - 'Neil LeVecke (LMU) plays in the Long Beach State vs Loyola Marymount match, score 11-7', by Chris Hunkeler, (2 Sep 2016). Available at [https://www.flickr.com/photos/chrishunkeler/31377652994] under a Creative Commons Attribution - ShareAlike 2.0 Generic. Full terms at http://creativecommons.org/licenses/by/2.0.

Page 161 - 'Hungary vs Holland water polo match at the XXII Olympiad, Moscow, 1980', by Vladimir Vyatkin, (10 Jul 1980). Available at [https://upload.wikimedia.org/wikipedia/commons/7/7d/RIAN_archive_8772_Hungary_vs_Holland_water_polo_match.jpg] under a Creative Commons Attribution - ShareAlike 3.0 Generic. Full terms at http://creativecommons.org/licenses/by/2.0.

Page 165 - 'Determined to get the shot away', by Malcolm Slaney, (28 Oct 2017). Available at [https://www.flickr.com/photos/malcolmslaney/26227017439/] under a Creative Commons Attribution - 2.0 Generic. Full terms at http://creativecommons.org/licenses/by/2.0.

Page 168 - The trajectory of a skip or bounce shot. '[Wasserball Bären von Winterthur]', by Rio Werner Hauser, (28 Jan 2012). [See p.211). Available at [https://www.flickr.com/photos/traumbilder/6816442715/in/photolist-bom1d4-bokYjT-bokYsD-bom1kp-bom3Gg-bokYcH-bom1s2-bom3rR-bom15B-ypK9P-tkf7DC-bomeGT-bomg7a-bomfxB-bom9hr-bom4bx-bom81n-bom6he-bokWN4-bokWWD-bom6wt-bom3jK-bom1Ga-bom9xD-bokYQP-bom1z2-bom2En-bokZSp-bombWT-bomfn8-bomfbD-bomd5i-2CUi95-m2kbNU-bomfKK-bom7Sa-bom51x-bom8Mt-bom3zt-m2kNtb-DJUFXZ-DJUBrK-DADrAB-DbqmiR-DhMYsN-m2kNnQ-bomccZ-bom3Wp-bokYXv-bokXgB] under a Creative Commons Attribution - 2.0 Generic. Full terms at http://creativecommons.org/licenses/by/2.0.

Page 170 - 'Water Polo played at Monmouth College water pool inside the Huff Center, UK', by Monmouth College, (5 Aug 2014). Licensed under the Creative Commons Attribution-Share Alike 4.0 International license.

Page 171 - 'Kostas Genidounias gets

ready to pass the ball off during the second quarter. The Trojans lead the score at half time 8-3. Genidounias scored a total of five goals during the game', by Neon Tommy, (1 Dec 2012). Available at [https://www.flickr.com/photos/neontommy/8235570737/in/album-72157632145529709/] under a Creative Commons Attribution - 2.0 Generic. Full terms at http://creativecommons.org/licenses/by/2.0.

Chapter 10

Page 173 - 'Partido de Waterpolo en Jaén, España [#2131]', by Juan Fernández, (2 Dec 2007). Available at [https://upload.wikimedia.org/wikipedia/commons/5/5c/Water_polo-2.jpg] under a Creative Commons Attribution - ShareAlike 2.0 Generic. Full terms at http://creativecommons.org/licenses/by/2.0.

Page 175 - 'Goalie James Clark blocks an attempt at the goal. Clark blocked a total of four goals during the first half of the game', by Neon Tommy, (1 Dec 2012). Available at [https://www.flickr.com/photos/neontommy/8235569951/in/album-72157632145529709/] under a Creative Commons Attribution - 2.0 Generic. Full terms at http://creativecommons.org/licenses/by/2.0.

Page 177 - Water Polo at Lake Macquarie ICG 2014. Photo taken at the 2014 Lake Macquarie International Children's Games in December 2014', by moetaz attalla, (10 Dec 2014).. Available at [https://www.flickr.com/photos/110823585@N06/15801069618/in/photolist-q5hBuN-qjyUXW-pq69pR-pq5Xee-ppRors-pq5Nzv-7ZNeSB-qmM45s-qmM2mh-qmLXWw-q5qpEZ-pq5vTz-qmQbi2-q5oUwT-q5qcdV-q5hNVL-qjxXnC-q5gzk9-qjxUzJ-q5hbsf-q5h9BG-qmLr7q-q5gr2f-q5ggdw-q5ov7M-pq54QH-ppQzaU-q5pPTv-q5pGxD-pq4Tdv-q5gM3j-pq4QB8-qmL5wN-qmPsNt-q5g2zq-q5gBGq-qmKW9L-q5fWks-q5o444-qmPigH-q5nZNM-qmD4gz-q5gpf1-qjx6Dj-q5pe3P] under a Creative Commons Attribution - 2.0 Generic. Full terms at http://creativecommons.org/licenses/by/2.0.

Page 181 - 'Womens Water Polo at the World Swimming Championships, Melbourne 2007 [#2]', by Flying Cloud, (2007). Available at [https://www.flickr.com/photos/flying_cloud/466833587/in/album-72157600441218707/] under a Creative Commons Attribution - ShareAlike 2.0

Generic. Full terms at http://creativecommons.org/licenses/by/2.0.

Page 182 (top) - 'GBR Water polo goalkeeper' by openDemocracy, (2012). Available at [https://www.flickr.com/photos/opendemocracy/7684062760] under a Creative Commons Attribution - ShareAlike 2.0 Generic. Full terms at http://creativecommons.org/licenses/by/2.0.

Page 182 (bottom) - 'About to score', by Three Peanuts, (27 Apr 2015). Available at [https://www.flickr.com/photos/3peanuts/17108333379/] under a Creative Commons Attribution - 2.0 Generic. Full terms at http://creativecommons.org/licenses/by/2.0.

Page 183 - 'Lake Macquarie International Children's Water Polo Games', by moetaz attalla, (10 Dec 2014). Available at [https://www.flickr.com/photos/110823585@N06/15802567289/in/photolist-q5qhGH-aAD9Tx-dxKspc-76naDw-dDM2V2-dP9SST-9sjAG3-4wWRBJ-q5h1V7-qmQqhe-pq5efp-9sjzXj-pq6G8R-pq4vxB-qhYcUs-q3MsjP-q5gJLy-q5q9qa-ppRHWE-qmLgZN-qmR3tH-q5pVk2-q5oBCn-q5hURJ-qmPZ2e-qjyg8h-q5fJcb-q5r2Kp-qmKAiJ-qmEXXV-QPz3Y4-RauRDh-QPz4Rg-FneQpi-23EfTAe-23EfTEx-FneQkv-23EfSoK-23WCcDu-23EfSrk-23EfTNt-23WCcpS-23WCc41-23EfTLz-FneQwT-23WCcAJ-23WCd3f-23WCd6w-23EfUgn-23EfTWz] under a Creative Commons Attribution - 2.0 Generic. Full terms at http://creativecommons.org/licenses/by/2.0.

Chapter 11

Page 187 - 'Romania psyching up prior to the USA v Romania match at the London Olympic Games', by Alex Lomas, (31 July 2012). Available at [https://upload.wikimedia.org/wikipedia/commons/a/ac/Romania_water_polo_team_huddle.jpg] under a Creative Commons Attribution - ShareAlike 2.0 Generic. Full terms at http://creativecommons.org/licenses/by/2.0.

Page 192 - 'Zach Gleason (LMU) and Lee Griffin (LB) play in the Long Beach State vs Loyola Marymount match, score 11-7', by Chris Hunkeler, (undated). Available at [https://www.flickr.com/photos/chrishunkeler/32110281171/in/photolist-ajxThK-R3zziu-QVtc62-PPDUV1-QwLmty-QVtzTr-R6X6zk-PPDRZ1-R3zyo3-PSmYCM-QwL67m-dxKs86-dxKrYV] under a Creative

Commons Attribution - ShareAlike 2.0 Generic. Full terms at http://creativecommons.org/licenses/by/2.0.

Page 193 - 'Water polo match between the national teams of the USSR and Hungary. The Soviet team won 5-4, at Lenin Central Stadium's swimming pool, XXII Olympic Games. (Eugeny Grishin (#4-RUS) and Istvan Szivos (#2-HUN) fighting for a ball)', by Alexander Makarov, (1 July 1980). Available at [https://upload.wikimedia.org/wikipedia/commons/a/a1/RIAN_archive_421039_Water_polo._USSR_vs._Hungary.jpg] under a Creative Commons Attribution - ShareAlike 3.0 Generic. Full terms at http://creativecommons.org/licenses/by/2.0.

Page 195 - 'Water Polo Hole', by Ryanjo, (4 Jul 2006). Available at [https://en.wikipedia.org/wiki/File:Waterpolohole.jpg] under a Creative Commons Attribution - ShareAlike 3.0 Generic. Full terms at http://creativecommons.org/licenses/by/2.0.

Page 196 - 'Womens water polo game at the Athens Olympic Games, 2004', by Maksim, [Prisonblues], (2004). Available at [https://commons.wikimedia.org/wiki/File:Waterpolo_man_up.jpg] under a Creative Commons Attribution - ShareAlike 3.0 Generic. Full terms at http://creativecommons.org/licenses/by/2.0.

Page 197 - 'Frame extracted from miniDV movie taken May 2005 at a high school water polo match', by Ryanjo, (8 Apr 2006). Available at [https://upload.wikimedia.org/wikipedia/en/archive/0/05/20060704191758%21Water_

Polo_Eggbeater.jpg] under a Creative Commons Attribution - ShareAlike 3.0 Generic. Full terms at http://creativecommons.org/licenses/by/2.0.

Page 200 - 'The bronze medal match between Greece (winners) and Italy (blue caps) at the 16th FINA World Championships, Kazan, Russia', by Oleg Bkhambri (Voltmetro), (8 Aug 2015). Available at [https://upload.wikimedia.org/wikipedia/commons/c/cf/Kazan_2015_-_Water_polo_-_Men_-_Bronze_medal_match_-_057.JPG] under a Creative Commons Attribution - CC0 1.0 Universal Public Domain Dedication. Full terms at http://creativecommons.org/licenses/by/2.0.

Page 202 - 'Water Polo at Athens Olympic Aquatic Centre', by Vchristos, (Aug 2004). Available at [https://en.wikipedia.org/wiki/Water_polo_at_the_Summer_Olympics#/media/File:Athens_Olympic_Aquatic_Centre_(1).jpg] and is in the Public Domain by permission of the Author.

Appendices

Page 210 - 'The bronze medal water polo match at the 16th World Championships, between Team Greece and Team Italy', by Oleg Bkhambri (Voltmetro), (8 Aug 2015). Available at [https://upload.wikimedia.org/wikipedia/commons/0/03/Kazan_2015_-_Water_polo_-_Men_-_Bronze_medal_match_-_094.JPG] under the Creative Commons CC0 1.0 Universal Public Domain Dedication.

Page 214 - 'USC Men's Water Polo 2012 NCAA National Champions, by Neon Tommy, (2012). Available at [https://www.flickr.com/photos/neontommy/8240269106/in/photolist-dyawVh-S1tr9-gcxVU9-aJtLrP-aA6TUX-7Ny1tn-UJyh3-7VxMh1-V546U-U5SD6s-7NBZeN-6YVMzM-pUFKvU-7LSVkn-dyazLS-cHMwd1-cQVLCb-HfBr9-8akiv6-W338ND-aAkDRE-dy583e-dy56dp-dxKrQF-dy57BB-cHMvVL-W61rLT-kyZkdA-7deyVL-596TGP-8MCke2-8MCkoV-qc4Dki-kiiE7N-dxQURQ-mLHhYY-neq76C-dtwYpm-8MBPFP-dyawtb-gcykjq-9ywUVg-rEKEGC-dy568D-9yzzJ9-qceKGa-dxKs5i-cExPLA-dxKrKK-7LWT9G] under a Creative Commons Attribution - ShareAlike 2.0 Generic. Full terms at http://creativecommons.org/licenses/by/2.0.

Back Cover - 'Looking to slot the pass. (2017-10-26-18-00-06.jpg), by Malcolm Slaney, (26 Oct 2017). Available at [https://www.flickr.com/photos/malcolmslaney/37929062812/in/photolist-8FaGsH-8zT5t7-kuERyM-9yzugo-dKUQj4-pUEJQq-6y4Vp7-dstDcU-8FaGra-59CRRe-6xZBBB-aAD8xR-gcxW1n-eWSM5P-kuG8m7-kuG7Uq-6xZqVX-7Mgpyt-2QTAKk-ZPCNbU-gcyDNt-ZQTbPk-pAh8Yo-W7MPf-pftVGv-kuGaRC-ZNamEQ-dy583e-8FaG2M-9yzWEC-pffuuy-9N5nNB-ZUmwoi-cHEVif-aAD2mi-gcytWz-gcyb4d-aAD1jD-dy56dp-8MBQ8H-5mQaZw-7Mgp7M-ZMEmWQ-dhLq8d-kuEPh2-ZKCjxG-gcyquA-cdq8G3-W4TAK-pffwfh] under a Creative Commons Attribution - 2.0 Generic. Full terms at http://creativecommons.org/licenses/by/2.0.

'USC Men's Water Polo 2012 NCAA National Champions, by Neon Tommy, (2012). [See p.213].

CPSIA information can be obtained
at www.ICGtesting.com
Printed in the USA
LVHW071653040122
707833LV00006B/148

9 780994 201416